A Promise in the Storm

Refusal to love is the only lasting death.
Beloved, rise and I shall meet you.

—*N. M.*

Genuine recycled paper with 10% post-consumer
waste. Printed with soy-based ink.

Nihil Obstat: Rev. Jack L. Krough
               Censor Librorum
               9 March 1996
Imprimatur: †Most Rev. John G. Vlazny, DD
               Bishop of Winona
               12 March 1996

The nihil obstat and imprimatur are official decla-
rations that a book or pamphlet is free of doctrin-
al or moral error. No implication is contained
therein that those who have granted the nihil obstat or imprimatur agree with the contents, opin-
ions, or statements expressed.

The publishing team included Michael Wilt, development editor; Barbara Allaire and Stephan
Nagel, consulting editors; Jeffrey Brodd and
Robert Smith, FSC, consultants; Rebecca Fairbank,
copy editor; Barbara Bartelson, production editor
and typesetter; Maurine R. Twait, art director;
Kent Linder, photo researcher; Nancy Marrocco,
chapter opening paintings; Tim Foley, illustrations;
and Jean-Claude Lejeune, black-and-white photo-
graphs.

The acknowledgments continue on page 203.

Printed in the United States of America

Printing: 9 8 7 6 5 4 3 2 1

Year: 2005 04 03 02 01 00 99 98 97

ISBN 0-88489-366-9

Saint Mary's Press
Christian Brothers Publications
Winona, Minnesota

A Promise in the Storm

Grieving & Dying with Hope

Nancy Marrocco

Contents

Appendices

1
The World of Saint Monica's High

Shared suffering, shared fear make a stronger bond than blood. Pain cracks us wide open and is totally revealing, and this is when we learn whom we really love and this is what we never forget.

—Agnes de Mille

A Gift and a Storm

George Freedon was tall, six feet six to be exact, and strangely handsome under his heavy, dark-framed glasses. His eyes were intense, yet disarming in their gentleness. At Saint Monica's High School he was known as Father George, the one who laughed a lot, the one with the big heart.

It was an autumn evening, a Friday. Father George was buckling up his briefcase, finally ready to go home for the day. As he was getting his keys out of his pocket, he caught sight of a small gift-wrapped package topped with a gold bow. His day had been hectic. He hadn't noticed the package, but then, it was a small package, practically hidden among the many books on his top shelf. Reaching up to get the gift, he couldn't help wondering who had put it there, and why. After all, it wasn't even close to his birthday.

He carefully undid the gold ribbon and lifted a curious-looking object out of its white tissue wrapping. It was what his students called a sand picture. As Father George tilted the frame this way and that, reds and blues and oranges swirled softly inside the glass. With each tiny tilt of the frame, something new took shape inside: at one moment, a calm lake; a second later, a big storm. For a moment, mesmerized by the changing flow of color and mood, Father George was unaware of his fatigue, unaware that it was nearly six o'clock.

The keys were still in his hand as he sank down into his big armchair by the door. Father George's armchair was well known throughout the school; it was the largest armchair any of the students had ever seen. But then, in order to fit Father George's tall frame, it had to be. He leaned back into his chair and propped up the sand picture on his knee. As he did, he watched the blending blues and light reds sinking softly to rest. The picture of stillness and calm carried Father George to a story of a night about two thousand years ago.

It was the night of a storm that nearly destroyed a boatload of people on a lake. It was the night of a storm—and a miracle. Amid the terror on the small craft, Someone had risen up to take charge of the wind and the sea. Someone had commanded the storm to die down. And it had.

The colors inside the fine black frame were now completely still. Looking more closely, Father George noticed the faintest hint of rose-pink tinging the dark blues. He felt a familiar comfort in that rose-pink. It was the same comfort he felt whenever he recalled the story of Jesus calming the sea, the story of the miracle at night.

Violent storms had often swept Father George's soul, storms of anger, of sorrow, of grief. The most furious upheaval and heaviest devastation had come with the death of his father, Charles Freedon. He had died after three years of being ravaged by Alzheimer's, a degenerative illness of the brain. Alzheimer's is particularly painful for those nearest its victims. George Freedon watched his beloved father lose first his memory, then his primary mental and physical functioning, and, finally, his dignity. Sometimes Charles recognized his son. Often he did not. Many times, at the foot of his father's bed, George buried his head in his hands and cried. His father stared into oblivion.

Father George had shed more tears during his father's illness than ever before in his life. In fact, it was during those three long years that Father George learned to cry. The son's journey through his father's dying was both grief and grace. The two go together. You see, Father George did not grieve alone. God was present. With grace had come the quieting of Father George's inner storms. In moments of intense anguish, Someone had risen up from the aching depths of his being.

Father George knew who had risen in his midst, just as the people on the boat had known. Relieved and stunned, those people had fallen to their knees with nothing but a whisper, "Surely this is the Son of God." Father George spoke the same words in the silence of his heart.

The Inner Rising

Father George sighed aloud. In his lap, the colors of the sand picture shifted gently, bringing him back to the present—and the lateness of the hour. He reminded himself that he must get home to rest, as the week had been long and challenging, filled with student counseling appointments. Despite his own proddings, though, he remained in the chair.

Father George ached for his students. As school chaplain, he daily heard stories of storms, of sadness and grief, from the young people of Saint Monica's. But it seemed that few of them had stories to tell of the calm. Not many ever talked about the inner rising of the Son of God, the person named Jesus. The few students who told of such things did so in private, never in a group. For Father George, it hurt to think that few recognized the One who rises—the One who, in his own rising, lifts us with him.

1
Saint Thomas More of England (1478–1535) said, "God came not to suppress suffering nor even to explain it, but to fill it with his presence." Write a paragraph connecting More's quote with Father George's experience of grief and grace.

Of course Father George knew that Saint Monica's was filled with good Catholic students. If a teacher were to ask, "What did Jesus do for us?" they could all answer, "He died for us." But did they understand what they were saying?

Take Keisha, for example. She was one of the students on his basketball team. Father George knew she was a spirited player, always working hard to improve herself both athletically and academically. But under pressure and sweating to make a shot, did her knowledge of Jesus make any difference to her?

He recalled last winter's semifinal. With the score tied and seconds left to play, Keisha had taken two foul shots. She missed both. Father George wondered, did Keisha know, in her heart, that Jesus was there with her on the basketball court? Did she know that as the buzzer sounded and the game was lost, the Risen Christ ached to love and console her?

Who Is Jesus?

Once again, Saint Monica's chaplain looked into the sand picture as if searching its depths for answers.

Who is Jesus? Over the course of his forty-two years, Father George had learned that Jesus Christ is not easily explained. Father George knew there was more to the mystery of Jesus than the mere fact that he had died. We all die. The mystery would not be explained even in that he was crucified. In Jesus' era, crucifixion was a common form of capital punishment. Nor would the mystery be explained in terms of Jesus' innocence. Many innocent people have been put to death. The answer would not be found in his being a caring person, because caring people have been around throughout history. Father George knew that he himself was a caring person, but that alone did not make him the Savior of the world! As he pondered silently, Father George smiled that wry little smile of his.

This priest knew that high school students are intelligent people. They could see that Jesus was not the only person who ever helped anyone, not the only person who ever suffered, and certainly not the only person ever to have died. How then, he asked himself, could they possibly appreciate Jesus' uniqueness?

Saddened, he looked at his sand picture. He turned it upside down. The reds, the blues, and the oranges fell quietly from the top. A new picture started to take shape. How he

2
Jesus asked his disciples, "'But who do you say that I am?'" (Mark 8:29). What would you say if he asked you the same question?

wished he could teach his students to reach for Jesus when their own joys and sorrows rose and fell. How he wished he could open their eyes to the truth of the One who rises. He longed for them to trust Jesus, who so long ago had lifted up that boatful of quaking, faint-hearted human beings. Gazing into the picture one last time, Father George saw something quite stunning in its beauty. He stared, transfixed. He couldn't look away.

Leaving his office that autumn night, Father George wondered who could possibly have left him such a gift, a carefully wrapped package topped with gold.

The Mystery of Jesus

He Loved the Unlovable

The following week, in a classroom near Father George's office, Veronica Shields was teaching her junior-year religion class. "When's the last time you said hello to someone you don't like?" she asked. "Who do you prefer to hang around with: the popular students or the so-called losers?"

Ms. Shields was working hard to lead her students to a discovery: that we like the people who like us. We are nicest to the people who are nicest to us. We are more drawn to people who look happy than to those who appear serious or down.

"Jesus welcomed all kinds of people."

Ms. Shields was contrasting our ways with the ways of Jesus Christ. "Jesus," she said, "was someone who welcomed all kinds of people, no matter how they looked or what they did. He made friends with the unpleasant, the diseased, the dirty, the unpopular, the dangerous, the untrustworthy. He made friends with people no one else would touch. He cared about people, even the ones who didn't agree with him, didn't support him, didn't understand him, didn't like him, accept him, or even speak to him."

As Ms. Shields spoke about Jesus, her students said nothing. Yet they couldn't help noticing a stark contrast between Jesus' attitude and that of most people at Saint Monica's. Most did not mix with people different from themselves, and they certainly did not speak kindly to anyone who rejected them. This is not to say that Saint Monica's was a bad crowd. On the contrary, despite their daily unkindnesses and human failures, Saint Monica's people were good people.

Ms. Shields's class was perplexed. These young people couldn't help wondering how Jesus could possibly be real. After all, how could anyone actually be nice to someone who hurt them?

Love, Even If You Die of It

Having caught her students' attention, Ms. Shields knew it was time to challenge them: "Let's say you've just come home with your hair newly cut and styled. You're feeling pretty good about yourself. Your brother laughs at you as you walk through the front door. How do you feel?" She paused. "What might you be tempted to say or do to your brother?

"How about this: One of your parents nags you—for the hundredth time—about your messy room. Can you resist the temptation to fire back an insulting remark? What if a fellow student embarrasses you in front of the whole class—how quick are you to grab the first opportunity for revenge? What if a friend talks about you behind your back—will you trust that friend again?" Ms. Shields paused. "Believe it or not, Jesus faced this same kind of abuse, particularly from his own best friends. But he never sought revenge."

Before she could open her mouth again, one of the students remarked: "But Jesus was God. Resisting that kind of stuff would've been easy for him." It was Simon who had spoken out. Simon was a serious student, one who spoke only on rare occasions. He was quick and to the point.

> "Jesus was human too! Being God didn't save him from the human struggle."

"Believe it or not, Simon, Jesus was human too, just as human as we are! Being God didn't save him from the human struggle. It was just as hard for him to resist temptation as it is for me or you. Jesus experienced intense anger, and he spoke freely in that anger. But—I'll say this again—he never sought revenge." As she expected, Simon did not contest her reply. Instead, he thought it over silently.

Another student continued where Simon had left off: "But when you read the Bible, Jesus seems to be doing great things all the time, curing people and making big speeches and all that."

Ms. Shields answered: "On the surface, it does appear that way, but when you read into the stories a little more deeply, you see his humanness. The Gospels don't go into a lot of detail about Jesus' inner feelings, but that doesn't mean he didn't have them.

"The Gospels don't point out how his heart might have been pounding when someone threatened him with hostile questions. They don't mention how excited he might have gotten when someone actually expressed interest in what he was teaching. They don't tell how hard he found it to control his temper when someone laughed in his face, or how hurt he felt when someone made fun of him behind his back. We often hear about his addressing the crowds. But we never hear about the anxiety he might have felt standing in front of a bunch of people who were just waiting to jump on him for the slightest mistake."

Playing idly with the chalk in her hand, Ms. Shields added, "Jesus felt whatever feelings you're feeling right now." Ms. Shields stopped talking. She did that whenever her students were really listening.

Ms. Shields knew her next statement would catch them by surprise; with it, she was certain of getting their fullest attention. "Just think—being human, there must have been times when, in the company of someone he cared about and to whom he felt attracted, Jesus desired sexual intimacy." The room was completely silent as she paused again. Then she said, "Instead of going into detail about all these kinds of things, the Bible simply says, 'Ours is not a high priest unable to sympathize with our weaknesses, but one who has been tested in every way as we are, only without sinning'" (Hebrews 4:15).

After a thoughtful moment, Ms. Shields concluded: "Have you ever noticed how often the Gospels tell of Jesus going away somewhere to pray alone? Can you guess why? The frustrations, hurts, and disappointments of the average day must have left him discouraged and down. Being human, he likely sought prayer because he needed to think through his problems, vent his hostilities, and cry out his hurts, and he needed to do this in the presence of God, his Father."

Keisha and Jerome

The clock struck eleven. The noise level in the room rose sharply with books closing, chairs scraping, and a million conversations happening at once. As usual, Ms. Shields's students filed quickly out of the room. (Students are always much faster getting out of a classroom than getting into it.) One of the young people, Jerome, was agitated. He wanted to catch up with Keisha. But she was already out the door and well on her way.

Jerome and Keisha had been going together since the Spring-into-Summer Dance last year. The first few months of their relationship had been like heaven, but in the past few weeks, all that had begun to change. As the crowd flowed out into the busy hallway, Jerome understood Ms. Shields's portrait of the Jesus who suffered frustration and disappointment. In his recent experience with Keisha, Jerome was feeling plenty of both.

The biggest problem between Jerome and Keisha had to do with her childhood dream of becoming a doctor. Jerome had been helping Keisha with chemistry since the beginning of the semester. They both knew she needed top grades to be accepted into a premedical program. Jerome craved Keisha's success; he liked the prestige and financial security associated with medicine. However, despite Jerome's enthusiasm and optimism about her professional goal, Keisha remained firmly realistic about the difficulties of what she had undertaken.

Keisha had been preoccupied before taking last week's chemistry exam. She knew it would be a tough one. Her chemistry teacher, notorious for giving the hardest tests at the beginning of the term, was known as the Exterminator. To make matters worse, basketball took up a lot of her time. But she loved it too much to quit. And Jerome, though supportive, demanded a lot of her attention. All things considered, Keisha knew that failing the chemistry exam was a real possibility.

> **Jerome stared down at the broken flowers. He was shaking.**

The night before the exam, Keisha's fears escalated. She phoned Jerome and asked him to come over. She met him at her front door, explaining, "Jerome, my gut tells me I'm going to fail this exam."

Her blunt statement made him see something he hadn't seen before: He needed her success to bolster his own hopes about their bright future together. Her being a physician was his dream not only for Keisha but also for himself. Falling back against her front door, Jerome felt confused, scared, and angry.

His next words to Keisha were a surprise, even to himself: "Then why don't you give up now? Forget chemistry. Forget the exam. Why go through all this if you're going down anyway? Maybe you're cut out for something totally different than this. As your friend, I can't allow you to go through with this."

She took a step back from him. Her eyes grew wide. Her mouth tightened into a hard line. Then, in a low voice she said, "Jerome, you really don't know me at all."

As she disappeared into the bathroom, she slammed the door behind her. A dried-flower wreath fell to the floor. Jerome stared down at the broken flowers. He was shaking. He knew she would study chemistry all night. He feared she might never speak to him again. Grim-faced, he left.

Since then a whole week had gone by, and Jerome and Keisha had not spoken to each other. Ms. Shields's classroom was empty. Locker doors crashed shut as students rushed to their next class. Jerome watched Keisha disappear from sight.

Alone and Abandoned

Father George had guessed that Ms. Shields was the source of the sand picture. She was a trusted colleague and a good friend. So when he asked her about it, he was surprised to find the gift had not come from her. In the course of their conversation, Father George asked, "These kids—what do they really think about Jesus?"

"Ask them," she shot back, a twinkle in her eye.

Several days later, Father George strode into Ms. Shields's religion class. He was wearing a bulky, hand-knit sweater, consisting of at least seventeen different colors. The students were glad to see him. Ms. Shields leaned against a side blackboard. She often did that, usually ending up covered in chalk dust and never seeming to mind.

Father George decided to tell a story about someone who failed regularly—Saint Peter. Father George smiled inwardly knowing that someone like Peter could be deemed a saint!

3

Read Mark 8:31–33. Write a paragraph discussing how Peter must have felt when hearing his friend Jesus predict Jesus' own execution. Has anything ever made you feel the way Peter must have felt? If so, write a second paragraph describing that experience.

After some one-liners and playful banter with the students, Father George perched himself on the corner of an empty desk and leaned into his story. "One time, Jesus was telling some of his friends about the fate in store for him. He said it straight out: that he would have to endure great sufferings; that he would be rejected by the elders, chief priests, and scribes; that he would be put to death; and that he would be raised on the third day.

"Peter was upset to hear his good buddy Jesus predicting his own suffering and death. Good old Peter—as usual, he just didn't get it! He didn't understand that it would be *necessary* for Jesus to suffer and die. So his immediate reaction was to rebuke Jesus, which means that Peter came down on Jesus like a ton of bricks. Peter insisted that such a disastrous fate shouldn't have to happen to someone as good as Jesus."

Hoping the students would see through Peter's seemingly noble defense of Jesus, Father George prodded them, "Can any of you see what's really going on with Peter, underneath those high-sounding words of his?" No one ventured an answer.

Father George continued. "Peter was mad—and worried. He had left everything to follow Jesus, had set all his hopes on Jesus' success in the world. He hadn't banked on this success including any kind of hardship, downfall, or disgrace. How could Peter hold up his own head if Jesus were publicly rejected? How could Peter bear to watch his friend suffer and die?

"But Jesus knew, deep down, that he had to go through what was coming. He knew that his would not be a worldly success, but a victory of another kind. Jesus knew he must not seek escape from the kind of death he was to die. How do you think Jesus felt about Peter's outburst?"

A student called out, "Doesn't the Bible say something or other about Satan at this point?"

"You've got it, Juan." Father George was pleased to get a reply. "Jesus' reaction to Peter's scolding was vehement— Jesus was just boiling! Jesus knew his mission was going to be really tough, but he had accepted it as his Father's will. Jesus looked straight at Peter and said: 'Out of my sight, Satan. You think as people think, not as God thinks.'"

Father George's eyes narrowed ever so slightly, and he smiled that little smile the students always noticed whenever he was about to say something really important. "Jesus erupted. He called Peter Satan because Peter was trying to take him away from doing God's will. . . . How do you think Peter reacted to this unexpected outburst from his Lord and Savior—from his best buddy—Jesus?"

The class puzzled silently. Father George loved this kind of moment. The students waited, half hoping that this kind-hearted priest would fill in the answer for them. He did not.

Instead, he asked another question. His eyes narrowed even further, so they knew the second question would be really tough: "What do you think Jesus felt inside as he watched one of his best friends and most ardent followers take on the role of Satan?" The class realized Father George was not going to answer this question for them either. For a long time, no one spoke. Finally, Keisha answered. In a steady voice she said aloud, "Jesus felt totally abandoned and alone."

Father George turned to Keisha. He saw suffering in her eyes.

Keisha continued: "Jesus must have known what he had gotten himself into. He knew it was going to be hard. But he had to do it. His decision had already been made." Hostility rose in Keisha's voice. "What Jesus needed was the support of his friends, not their spineless whining that he should just back off. He was left to face an uphill climb alone because his so-called friend Peter was too weak even to understand him. Jesus must have felt so alone. Peter did exactly the opposite of what Jesus wanted him to do. I bet Jesus just wanted to get away from Peter."

"Keisha, you're describing something more than just aloneness," Father George challenged.

She looked into his eyes but could not speak.

Jerome, at the back of the room, heard Keisha's words as if they had been aimed directly at him. He felt ashamed about trying to talk her out of medical school. He had not realized that a feeling of aloneness had been at the root of her violent reaction to him. He had thought he was helping take some of the pressure off her. Father George's suggestion about something more than aloneness was no puzzle for Jerome. Jerome knew what the "something more" was: Keisha was angry, very angry. Jerome feared more than ever that he had lost Keisha for good.

Jesus the Risk Taker

Father George was delighted to see the hand of yet another student go up. That student was confused: "But I thought

Peter and Jesus stayed friends right to the end of the Bible. . . . How did they ever get together again if Jesus actually felt that bad about Peter?"

Father George responded by asking, "Do you think Jesus was tempted to dump Peter?"

He noticed that Keisha lowered her eyes.

Father George continued: "Sure he was tempted. But he didn't dump Peter. In fact, Jesus kept running risks by telling the truth, especially to his best friends."

Ms. Shields spoke up: "It's so hard for us to be nice to people when they do things we don't want them to do! This is the very point I was trying to make the other day. I admit I find this to be one of the hardest things in life. For me, the amazing thing about Jesus is that he forgave his friends for rejecting him, even without getting an apology from them. Jesus resisted the temptation to get revenge, even though lashing out probably would have felt safer than reaching out. I don't mind telling you that I've fallen into the trap of getting revenge, and I've hurt people because of it. It really is hard to forgive, to trust again."

Ms. Shields had no way of knowing about the situation between Jerome and Keisha. However, both of them heard their teacher loud and clear. Jerome was feeling guilty. No wonder Keisha had been avoiding him. He didn't know how this mess would ever get worked out.

Keisha knew she'd find it hard to trust Jerome again, hard to be honest with him again about her worries—and her dreams. Jesus never abandoned his friends, though that meant he risked getting hurt again. Keisha wasn't sure she'd take a risk like that.

Keisha felt alone with her anxiety about medical school. Could she, like Jesus, trust a God she couldn't see? She found it particularly hard to believe in God when she was feeling down. But what she had been hearing was that Jesus kept searching for God even when he felt no sense of God's presence, even when he had no hope at all. Jesus stayed faithful even when his mission looked ridiculous and insane. Jesus did what he knew to be right, regardless of the cost.

Keisha wondered, could she?

His Dying Breath

Once again, it was almost dismissal time. Ms. Shields distributed sheets of blue paper and announced this assignment: "Read this sheet next time you feel rejected." At home that night, Keisha read her blue sheet. As she did, she pulled her black kitten into her lap. This is what she read:

As Jesus died, he did something that human persons often fail to do: He loved in the face of rejection. He loved the people who spat in his face and made fun of him, even those who called themselves his friends and then left him to die. The Scriptures, proclamations of this extraordinary love, pull us deeper into the mystery of Jesus, deep enough to picture his very soul: "At noon darkness came over the whole land until three in the afternoon. And at three o'clock Jesus cried out in a loud voice, *'Eloi, Eloi, lema sabachthani?'* which is translated, 'My God, my God, why have you forsaken me?'" (Mark 15:33–34).

> Father, a wall of fear is in my face. I ache.
> > Dark fog is all around. I am deserted, even by you.
> Father, in death, I have only one gift left to give: my love.
> I choose to love those who have broken my heart
> > and ripped it out.
> I will climb the heights of heaven to give this gift.
> I will eat the dust of the earth.
> I will go where my God leads me.
> Father, tear down in me all that prevents
> > my loving them at this moment of agony.
> Make me to trust, even though I stand utterly alone
> > against the world and all that's in it.
> In death, O God,
> > with the dust of death in my mind, in my heart,
> > in my veins, and in my mouth, I beg you:
> > take my Light and give it to them that they might see.
> > Take my Love and give it to them,
> > even as I hang destroyed.
> > This, Father, is my gift: raise my people from this grave.
> My Lord and my God, I am utterly in your hands.

"Then the veil of the temple was torn down the middle. Jesus cried out in a loud voice, 'Father, into your hands I commend my spirit'; and when he had said this he breathed his last" (Luke 23:45–46).

Keisha's black kitten had fallen asleep in her lap. Keisha did not understand many things about Jesus. However, one thing was clear to her as she closed her eyes: she wanted to love as he loved. In her arms, she cradled the sleeping kitten. She resolved that she would try to talk to Jerome again before the end of the week.

Jerome had left his blue sheet on his desk at school. He neither missed it nor thought of it again.

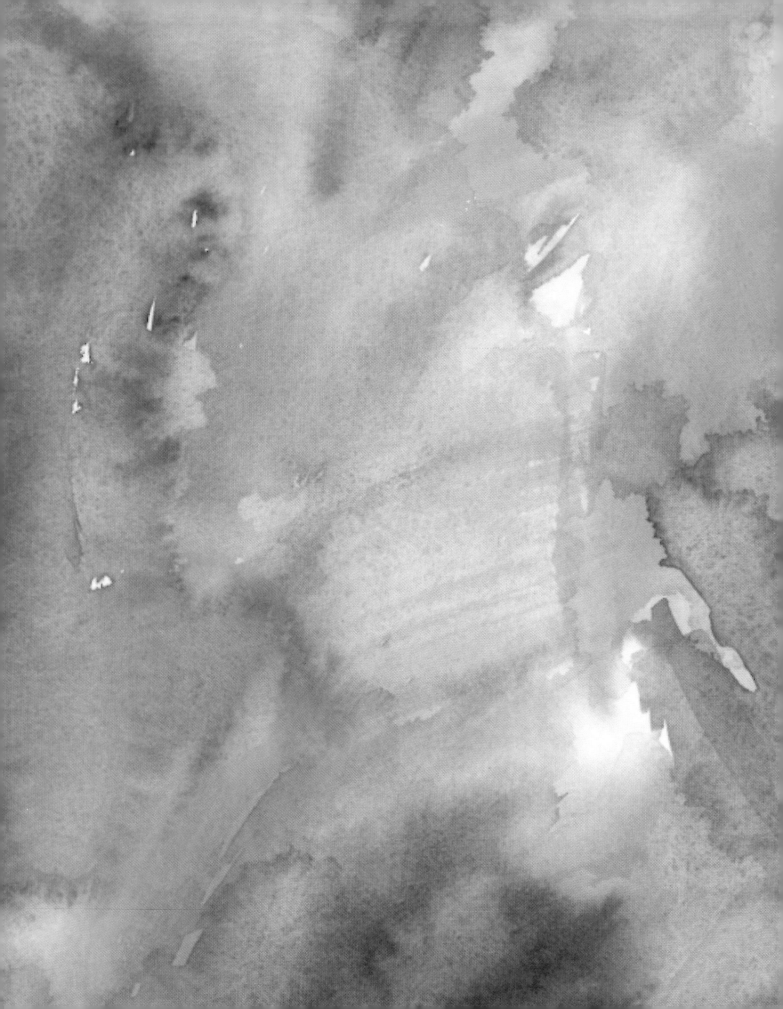

2 Denying Death's Reality

"Dying," he said to me, "is a very dull dreary affair." Suddenly he smiled. "And my advice to you is to have nothing whatever to do with it," he added.
—Somerset Maugham, just before his death in 1965, as recorded by his nephew, Robin Maugham

Death: No Neutral Ground

You've just met some of the faculty and students of Saint Monica's High School. You've met Father George and Veronica Shields, Jerome and Keisha, and a few of the others. This book tells their story. Saint Monica's is probably a lot like your school. It's made up of people who try hard and care a lot, people who make mistakes, people who get hurt, people who are in love, people who are searching for answers, people with all kinds of problems, people with all kinds of dreams and hopes, people with all kinds of questions.

Saint Monica's is exactly like your school in one very significant way; everyone at Saint Monica's will someday die—though they don't know when or how—and every single one of them will grieve the loss of another. Any book about people's lives is also a book about death.

Death is a subject that evokes strong feelings. How do you feel about the subject of death? If you're like the Saint Monica's crowd, you probably don't spend a whole lot of time thinking about it. Occasionally people have bad dreams about dying, read about a tragic accident, or see a movie about death. Then they talk about it—but only a little, and not for very long. And some of them have already experienced the death of someone close. To most people, most of

1
Have you ever thought about your own death?

2
"When a person is born we rejoice, and when they're married we jubilate, but when they die we try to pretend nothing has happened" (Margaret Mead). Write a page-long essay reflecting on this observation.

the time, though, death seems remote, unthinkable, or even impossible—that is, of course, until death strikes, as it always does.

When the subject of death is raised, what feelings arise in you—sadness? fear? anger? confusion? powerlessness? despair? curiosity? At Saint Monica's, almost everyone fears death; some are fascinated by it; and all are curious, at least secretly. The faculty and students have lots of questions about death: Why do we have to die? Is there an afterlife? Is there really a God? Does God really love us, and if so, why does God allow people to die? Why must innocent people suffer?

What are your questions?

Unasked Questions

Whatever their fears or fascinations, though, most of the people at Saint Monica's don't talk much about death. Their questions are profoundly intelligent and important, but they usually don't ask their questions, at least not out loud. Instead, they go about their lives as if there were no such thing as dying. As Woody Allen once put it: "I'm not afraid to die. I just don't want to be there when it happens."

Evading and denying death is pretty common, and not just at Saint Monica's High School. The very same kind of evasion and denial is found in the hospital on the other side of town, in government offices, and in neighborhoods around Saint Monica's. It has been that way for generations. This denial is deeply rooted and pervasive in our world.

To really understand the people at Saint Monica's, to really get into their story, you must understand the far-reaching effects of death denial. This denial shapes their lives—the way they think and act, what they hope and dream. This same denial shapes your life, too. The big problem is that denying death doesn't make it go away. We still have to face death. We still have to grieve, and we still have to die. It's difficult to do that in a culture that constantly takes flight from the truth about death.

The Growth of Cultural Attitudes

To help us understand our cultural denial of the reality of death, let's explore *how* cultural attitudes develop. The story of Sarah Spencer, a junior at Saint Monica's, shows us how these attitudes grow.

Sarah's Story

Sarah is a product of her culture. She hates to cry, especially in front of her peers. She always has. Sarah is like most of us. Whether at a funeral, a wedding, or a movie, we tend to choke back the tears. When it happens, on occasion, that someone breaks down and cries out loud, chances are that someone else will rush in quickly to put a stop to the tears.

The problem is that tears need to be cried. In Sarah's case, this need became particularly urgent when she was in third grade. Her parents had been fighting with each other for months. They were headed for divorce. One day at school, unable to focus on arithmetic, Sarah felt tears welling up. Fearing someone might see her cry, she asked to go to the restroom. Hidden away behind a locked door in one of the stalls, Sarah broke down. She cried and cried and cried.

After her parents divorced, Sarah's mother moved to a distant state and rarely made contact. Sarah and her father moved into a townhouse, and Sarah's widowed grandmother came to live with them. The move was good for Sarah's grandmother, who disliked living alone. And the move was very good for Sarah. She came to love her grandmother as if her grandmother had been her own mother.

Sarah's grandmother was diagnosed with cancer at the start of Sarah's sophomore year. For Christmas that year, she gave Sarah her gold wedding ring as a keepsake. In the midst of Sarah's sorrow over her grandmother's illness, the ring became a treasure. It was rarely off her finger, until one day the following spring. Sarah was working with clay in the art room and had taken off the ring to keep it safe. But she lost it.

An "Innocent" Rumor

Losing the ring was painful for Sarah. It reminded her of the absence of her mother, and it reminded her that her grandmother would soon be gone as well. Then, of all things, a rumor started. You surely know about rumors, how mean and ugly they can get. No doubt there have been rumors at your school. This one was about Sarah and her boyfriend, Mike. It all started more or less innocently, as most rumors do.

The day she lost the ring, just before getting on the bus to go home, Sarah told Mike what had happened. She was afraid she'd start crying if they kept talking about it, so they agreed not to sit together on the bus. Sarah sat at the back of the bus, and Mike sat closer to the front. A few minutes later, though, her tears started.

Nicole, a very popular student at Saint Monica's, saw Sarah crying at the back of the bus. Nicole also saw that Mike was not sitting with Sarah. Nicole seemed to notice everything.

As it happened, Nicole was interested in a guy named Matthew. Though she could have attracted just about any guy in the school, he was the only one she really wanted. Matthew always wore a black leather jacket, even when it was a little too warm for a jacket. And he always wore sunglasses, even when the sun really wasn't all that bright. Nicole had been looking for an opportunity to talk to Matthew. When Matthew got on the bus, Nicole whispered to him that Mike and Sarah must have had a fight.

The bus pulled away from the school. Matthew was always hungry for a little excitement, so he was intrigued to think that a fight could have broken out between two such "lovebirds" as Sarah and Mike. That night, watching a video with his longtime friend Jerome, Matthew mentioned his suspicion that Sarah Spencer was cheating on Mike, and that Mike must have found out.

As you can imagine, rumors about Sarah and Mike quickly grew and spread. Over the next few days, Sarah felt alienated and betrayed by the very people she had thought were her friends.

Collective Power Creates Culture

Sarah's story, showing how rumors get started, also teaches us how basic cultural beliefs get started. Just as rumors begin with small things, so do cultural teachings.

Each person who helped build the rumor about Sarah and Mike probably didn't feel he or she was doing anything wrong. However, all those seemingly harmless little conversations added up to a major problem for Sarah and Mike. This is how things often work in our world. Individually we may not realize the impact of our words and actions upon others. However, the effect is felt. Collective power takes shape.

Once a wrong becomes a collective wrong, a further problem develops. The individuals in the group no longer feel responsible for what has happened, and everyone feels

Just as rumors begin with small things, so do cultural teachings.

powerless to change what has already gone out of control. Even if Nicole realizes her mistake in starting the rumor, any effort to stop it is likely to be ineffective. No one can undo the damage.

The same principle holds true for cultural attitudes. The cultural reality of death denial is so deeply rooted and pervasive that it would be impossible for one person to put an end to it. We are all caught up in it, and even if we change our personal attitude toward death, we live in a society that constantly challenges our improved understanding.

The Positive Side of Collective Power

We must remember that just as we have collective power to do harm, we also have collective power to do good. Bad things like rumors are not the only kind of thing we can create together. Collectively we can accomplish good things too, great things, things that no one of us alone could ever begin to accomplish.

Take the annual Saint Monica's school play, for example. It's the biggest production of the entire year. The big and little efforts of many individuals working together bring about something quite spectacular.

The student actors on stage are obviously important to the play's success. But they would have little or no success without the huge offstage crew, each person carrying out a vital role in the production: costume design, makeup, lighting, ticket sales, and so on.

The combined efforts of the huge cast and crew bring about a successful dramatic presentation each year. If you were to walk into the cast party after the last show, you would be overwhelmed by the collective energy, excitement, and joy of all who took part.

Both the rumor about Sarah and Mike and the annual school play are illustrations of collective power. When we speak about our cultural beliefs and practices, we are speaking about something collective. The values, priorities, and actions of our culture are created and developed over time by the cumulative values, priorities, and actions of all the individual people who make up our culture. The rumor demonstrates our collective power for hurt; the play demonstrates our collective power for creativity.

Every culture evolves and lives by its own set of unwritten rules. In our culture, a basic rule is this: We must not look into the face of death.

Denying Death: What Our Culture Teaches Us

Now that we've gotten a glimpse at how our cultural attitudes develop, let's look at some of the things we learn from our culture about death and dying.

Growing Old Is Bad

You've already met Father George, and you know that his dad suffered from Alzheimer's disease. Father George used to visit his dad almost every day at Sunnyside Nursing Home. His dad shared a room with three other men on a ward filled with ailing, aged, incoherent, and broken-down men and women. George Freedon's father dribbled on his chin and bedclothes when he ate or drank. He wore diapers.

In our everyday travels, we don't bump into many people like Father George's dad. Aged and infirm people are often hidden from the rest of the world in institutions. We prefer not to see this evidence of our own mortality.

To make matters worse, we tend to disrespect those who are higher up in years. At Saint Monica's, for example, an elderly man once substituted for an absent teacher. Although the substitute was a gifted and competent teacher, the students assumed he was a pushover, someone who knew nothing, someone of whom they could easily take advantage. The increased learning, wisdom, and experience associated with aging are often no match for a culture that sees aging in a negative light.

It's no wonder that once people reach their thirties, many of them prefer not to reveal their age. Getting old is considered bad; the elderly are seen as being of no value.

Everything Must Age

Hiding the aging process leaves us with one obvious problem: Everything must age, and no matter how hard we try, we can't stop it. Aging is a fundamental truth of human existence. In fact, all things age. Think of the cross-trainers you buy in September. New, they look great. But with a year's wear, what happens to them?

Think about food. If you leave milk out of the refrigerator, it quickly sours. In fact, even if you never take it out of the refrigerator, you can't stop it from going sour. Most foods are highly perishable. Can you think of any food that will not eventually go bad?

Deterioration happens to just about everything. Even something as seemingly durable and unchangeable as rock is dramatically changed over time. Take a look down a deep rock-walled gorge and see how the force of water has gradually worn down the rock.

Humans age. As we do so, we steadily lose both our physical beauty and our physical prowess. A culture that denies its own mortality must work hard to exalt its youthful beauty and vigor. Regardless of our most artful denial, however, all things perish. This earth and these physical bodies of ours were simply not built to last forever. The world is a changing, passing place, and we are changing, passing beings.

Stay Beautiful, Young, and Fit

One way to avoid what we'd rather not see is to look at something else. To keep our mind off sickness, aging, and death, we focus on staying beautiful, fit, and young. This tactic is well illustrated by our media—television, video, cinema, radio, newspapers, magazines. The media focus our attention primarily on the young, the healthy, and the beautiful, rather than on those who are old, sick, and plain. Our cultural heroes are the good-looking young soap stars and the muscular sports figures in top physical condition. From an early age, we're taught that we need to look good to get ahead.

In recent years, we've discovered the far-reaching benefits of regular exercise. Being fitness-conscious is positive for our physical and emotional health and well-being. However, for some people, physical fitness becomes an end in itself. Inherent in this attitude is a subtle, unspoken, perhaps unconscious belief that we can keep our body young and active forever if we work out long enough and hard enough. Becoming fanatical about exercise can be a way of denying that our body will inevitably break down.

We set equally high standards for ourselves in terms of physical beauty. Consider Nicole, the student who started the rumor about Sarah and Mike. Nicole does her homework with the television on. Before her work is finished, she sees countless commercials. One tells her how to fight acne. Others tell her which brand of jeans will most flatter her shape, which shampoo will make her hair sexiest, and which lip gloss will net her the most exciting love life. All evening long, Nicole hears the same message over and over: To be successful in life, you have to look good. Setting her homework aside, she makes a shopping list.

Incredible though it sounds, the cultural admonition to look good extends even to the dead. Funeral homes dress up and decorate the body so that the deceased looks as good as possible. Cover-up creams and other types of makeup are used after death as well as before! We are very skilled at concealing blemishes and making the body appear beautiful, so much so that a corpse can look more like a sleeping body than a dead body.

We block ourselves from seeing the truth.

We have evolved into a consumer world in which we persuade ourselves that if we buy certain things, and continue to buy them, we can keep ourselves young, beautiful, and fit. We get the idea that if we work at it, we will never age or suffer.

3
How important are looks at your school?

Hide Your Emotional Weaknesses

In addition to telling us it is important to cover up physical weaknesses and imperfections, our culture tells us it's just as important to cover up emotional weaknesses and imperfections—our hurts, anxieties, sorrows, and failures. Why? Because they remind us of our limits. Sarah Spencer, you recall, hid her tears from her schoolmates. She couldn't bear for them to know that she was hurting, that her life was broken by her parents' marital problems. We don't like the fact that our emotions can stop us in our tracks and limit our power, so we do what we can to keep feeling good.

Never Admit Your Pain

If we are not feeling good, though, our culture teaches us that no one else wants to know about it. A strange thing happened at the height of the rumor about Sarah and Mike. Sarah was at her lowest point. She was on her way to school one morning. In passing, someone said to her: "Hi. How are you?" Sarah smiled and answered, "Fine, thank you!" Why in the world would Sarah smile and say she felt fine when her whole life was crashing down around her?

Denial of death begins with small denials, just as rumors begin with small misstatements. Society has taught Sarah that it's not okay to feel bad. So she just says what we all say—whether it's true or not—"Fine, thank you!" When we're down, most of us are not likely to admit how we're really feeling, except perhaps to the few people we really trust. Sarah had told no one but Mike about her grandmother's cancer and about the ring.

Most of the time we try to look as if we're succeeding at everything and have no problems. Sarah's story illustrates our common fear of appearing emotional or weak. We feel safer if we "put on a happy face." This is part of death denial. We dare not show how fragile we really are. Although it would be unwise for Sarah to pour out her heart to anyone and everyone, working so hard to conceal her feelings may lead to greater difficulties.

The danger is that when we hide our limits, we begin to believe that we should have no limits at all. We begin to believe that we should be impervious to pain. We deny our sore spots and our hurts. We don't learn to cry, and we don't learn to grieve.

And there's the problem, because death is the ultimate limit. Regardless of our hiding, death will find us all. We are

4
Do you cry? Do you cry in public? Write a page describing your attitude toward crying.

not impervious to it, and we cannot overcome it. A culture that hides from its own hurts, wounds, and limits is hiding from its own mortality and from its own human nature.

Feel Good All the Time

To feel good constantly, our culture encourages us to get rid of pain and get rid of it fast.

TV commercials had a powerful effect on Nicole. She stopped doing homework to make a shopping list. Advertising is a persuasive form of "cultural speech." It conveys the teachings of our culture. Think about the subway ads for a big concert, the huge picture of a cheeseburger and fries on the side of a bus shelter, the great sound equipment we hear about between songs on the radio, and the endless piles of junk mail. What is the message running through all this advertising? It is a promise: All these things can make you hap-

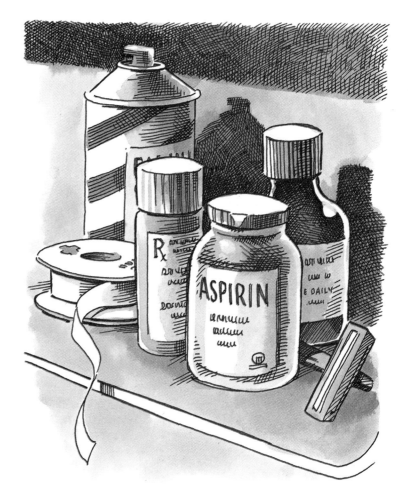

pier, sexier, stronger, more popular, and more successful. All these things can free you from suffering.

The voice of advertising may be subtle, but it's loud and distracting. We have painkillers to bring relief as soon as we get an ache. We have salty snacks and instant drinks to distract us whenever we're feeling down. All these keep us focused on our quest for enjoyment, leisure, and comfort, so that we can avoid noticing the pain of being human.

This isn't to say that medicine and food are, in themselves, bad things. They're good things. Frequently, though, we abuse them.

Sash was a freshman at Saint Monica's when he began taking an occasional aspirin for his headaches. He was a fragile, sometimes confused young person, and his freshman year was filled with new stresses. Before long, he was taking aspirin all the time. Then he discovered that by taking a few aspirin mixed with muscle relaxants from the family medicine cabinet, he was able to create strange physical sensations. Sash didn't find the resulting shakes and lightheadedness particularly pleasant, but they were better than getting in touch with what was really bothering him. For Sash, medication became an unhealthy escape. The more pills he took, the more pills he needed, and the more he sought escape of all kinds. He did not know that he had become seriously depressed. He was cut off from everyone, including his twin brother, Simon—and even himself. Sash's little escapes eventually produced grave consequences.

> To deny that our emotional pains exist is unhealthy.

Certainly we all have times when we need to minimize or distract ourselves from our emotional pains. But to deny that they exist is unhealthy and unrealistic. Doing so leads to the supposition that our humanness is an obstacle to a good life, and so we fight the supposed obstacle in more and more dangerous ways. By hiding our pain, too, we close off the possibility that through pain we will continue to grow and develop as human beings.

Do Not Talk About Death

During the average week, how often do you sit down with someone and talk about death? How often does the subject of dying come up when you're having lunch in the cafeteria, shopping for a new pair of jeans, or getting a ride somewhere?

In our culture, death is an unpopular topic. For the most part, death becomes part of conversation only when someone close dies. Even then, many people won't talk about it. Avoiding talk of death is an obvious form of denial.

A less obvious, but equally effective, form of denial is the use of euphemisms. Euphemisms obscure the subject so that we can speak about it in a less direct way. Euphemisms sugarcoat the truth. For example, it's more common to say, "My uncle passed away" than to say, "My uncle died." Or we say, "She's resting at the funeral home" or "She's gone to her eternal rest," avoiding the direct statement, "She died." Euphemisms are sometimes marked by humor. We might say, "He's six feet under" or "She's pushing up daisies" or "He kicked the bucket last week." Humor is a wonderful gift, but it can also be a sign of our denial of death.

So extreme is our death denial that our euphemisms extend even to animals. We say that our cat, Tiger, was "put to sleep" or that Casey, our dog, was "put down."

When we avoid *saying* things directly, we avoid *facing* them directly.

Keep Yourself Busy!

Busyness is a popular avoidance technique for a society that does not want to think about death. We live in an activity-oriented culture. We operate on the basis of schedules and timetables and calendars and clocks. Among Saint Monica's students, the person who has a part-time job and a heavily booked social calendar is thought to be successful and popular. Far less admired is the one who doesn't go out much, who spends time alone, and whose calendar is mostly unbooked. If asked, "How was your weekend?" the Saint Monica's crowd knows it's better to say, "Busy!" than "Didn't do much."

We value activity. We value busyness. And it's good to be active, to be involved, to exercise our talents, to create, to move forward. But busyness can become a problem. Why? Because it can lead to avoidance. The person who is always busy gradually takes less time to think, to question, to search, and to reflect on what's happening in life. Eventually the really busy person might not take the time to feel. This person might even be too busy to realize that he or she has actually lost the ability to feel.

Still, busyness is very attractive. Busyness offers something we all crave: distraction. When we are distracted, pain seems more escapable, life seems more controllable, and death seems less real.

5
Are you in danger of being too busy?

Seek Instant Gratification

Our culture teaches us that when we want something, we should expect it immediately. TV commercials tell us, "Don't wait until you have the money and can go to the mall—call the toll-free number *now,* use a credit card, and we'll ship it to you overnight!" When we get hooked on instant gratification of our desires, we start to lose the ability to deal patiently with life's many challenges.

We have all experienced the desire for instant gratification. Keisha stands in line at the donut shop. She wants a double chocolate cream. Her mouth is watering, and she finds it harder and harder to stand and wait. She is losing precious time. Keisha, like the rest of the Saint Monica's crowd, doesn't like delays.

We expect immediacy in all aspects of our life. With telecommunications we can quickly obtain whatever information we want—the ski report, the news, the weather, the stock market report. Matthew loves immediacy, especially the instant replays in football games. Right away, he gets a second chance to feel the excitement. Excitement and enjoyment, of course, are not bad things. But Matthew's love for immediacy goes too far— lacking instant gratification, he gets incredibly angry. He cannot bear an unmet need or an unfulfilled want.

> Our vulnerable nature is not a curse, but a very useful gift.

We are becoming a people who cannot bear to wait for anything, who are losing touch with the meaning of need and the value of searching, waiting, and hoping.

Dying has to do with being vulnerable and facing limits. Waiting, needing, searching, and hoping are necessary human experiences. The less able we are to wait, to feel an unmet need, or to be uncertain, the more difficult our struggle with issues of death will be. Underneath it all, we are vulnerable. As you hear more of what happens at Saint Monica's, you'll see how this vulnerable nature of ours is not a curse or an affliction, but a gift, and a very useful one at that.

Never Fall Silent or Still

Our culture encourages us to keep all our senses occupied. To fall silent or still often opens the mind to thoughts we'd rather not think. No wonder shopping is a favorite pastime. Go into any shopping mall, and you will be bombarded by all kinds of signs giving you all kinds of messages, by music coming from everywhere, by merchandise filling every corner of every shop, by wall-to-wall movement of people and things. In a shopping mall, you are not likely to experience silence or stillness.

6

Can you be silent with God?
Remain silent and inactive for
five minutes. See what happens.

When a teacher is talking to a class or someone is giving a presentation, everyone suddenly pays attention if the speaker stops talking, even briefly. A few seconds of silence are so dramatic simply because quiet is so uncommon.

How much silence can you manage before you have to get up and do something—turn on some music or channel surf or make a phone call?

A death-denying society finds silence threatening. In the silence we run some risks. We might feel boredom; we might feel something that hurts; we might ask ourselves questions we cannot answer; we might experience ourselves to be alone; we might think about dying. Our culture offers us many ways to avoid silence. Welcoming distractions is a popular way of banishing thoughts about dying.

The Illusion of Physical Immortality

How many times have you seen your favorite actor shot at close range? Did those bullets kill him, or did he live to make another movie, and another, and another? Of course we know that movies are not real life, and so we do not believe that the actor is actually in any danger. But movie and TV special effects are highly sophisticated. To hold our attention, the media try to keep us stimulated. Therefore, even though we are merely sitting in front of a screen, the scene we are viewing looks amazingly similar to a real fatal wounding and gruesome death. But soon after, we see that wounded and dead person alive and well, acting out some other story. Can you see what's happening? It's as if death has no effect—it doesn't even slow us down! Gradually, imperceptibly, we become desensitized to death.

In the faculty lounge at Saint Monica's High, the radio is on, giving morning rush hour traffic reports. This is what is said: "There's a multi-vehicle collision on the interstate, a car blocking the center lane on Lakeshore Avenue, and a minor mishap at Fourth and King." This is what is not said: "There are seven men and women bleeding on the interstate. Someone's fiancée is blocking the center lane on Lakeshore because she's slumped over the wheel, dying. And at Fourth and King, the consequences will be severe for the underage driver who took her parents' car without permission and smashed a headlight."

Of course news stations can't give us all the details, nor could we bear to hear them even if they could. What must be realized is that tragedy, anguish, and death happen every minute of every day, but we often speak of them as if they mean nothing. We speak of deaths as simple statistics. We are more and more desensitized.

We Think We Are All-Powerful

Our bookstores are filled with self-help books. The message at the heart of many of them is this: If we try hard enough and work at it long enough and keep using the right kind of approach, we can do just about anything. We have astonishing built-in healing mechanisms and an innate potential to transcend our own limits. And it is wise to tap in to these resources and use them to live a better life. Self-help books are a good tool for helping us tap in to and use these resources.

Yet in the midst of the best approaches and most persevering efforts, we inevitably come face-to-face with our own limits. We still suffer, and we still fail. We still gradually lose our abilities. We still get sick. We still age and die. We are not all-powerful, and self-help programs that try to convince us otherwise are not doing us a favor. They are simply supporting the denial of an important aspect of our human nature: We are limited, and to be fully human we must live to the fullest within those limits.

Death is the ultimate proof of our limitedness, our mortality, our creatureliness. And yet, without admitting it, our world functions as though it were its own endless source of power and life. A world that does not acknowledge its own limits will not acknowledge its own death. It is dangerous for a race of very limited human beings to function as though it had no limits at all.

What will happen to the death deniers at Saint Monica's when death strikes someone close, as it surely will?

3 Seeing Life in the Face of Death

*E*very parting gives a foretaste of death; every
coming together again a foretaste of the resurrection.
—Arthur Schopenhauer

The Price of Death Denial

The cultural denial of death brings with it three serious consequences:

- Death comes as a far greater shock than it otherwise might. Death in our culture leaves mourners feeling isolated and without hope, their world shattered.
- Mourners are unprepared for the hard but necessary work of grieving. After all, if dying has been a taboo topic, so has grieving. And the inability to enter into the experience of grief can cause real damage in individuals, families, and communities.
- Denial of death often goes hand in hand with denial of God. When human beings think of themselves as the source of their own life and power, faith is no longer valued. God is seen as irrelevant or nonexistent. Therefore, rather than standing with faith and looking into the face of death, those for whom God is irrelevant find themselves feeling alone in the face of death. In doing so, they may experience true terror.

Faith Makes a Difference

As you may recall, Father George received a sand picture as a gift. When he first looked at the ever-changing patterns made by the wet sand, he saw a calm lake turn into a fierce storm. Then he remembered the Bible story of Jesus' saving

presence in the storm. That story reminded Father George that he need not stand alone against death. He ached for his students. He didn't want them to stand alone in their times of sadness, suffering, frustration, and grief. He wanted them to know Jesus as Savior and Comforter. But with our cultural clamoring about avoidance and denial of death, it's no wonder Father George and Ms. Shields found their students so ambivalent about God and Jesus. After all, the cultural admonition is powerful and clear: Death is to be denied, suffering hidden, sickness and aging covered up, and the most disturbing questions never asked.

Jesus bluntly asked the toughest of questions and deliberately focused on the truth of things, even when that focus was painful or challenging. He neither evaded nor denied death. In fact, Jesus walked straight into death—consciously and willingly. He taught people to pass through death in order to find life, to learn how to suffer in order to find happiness. The Christian is willingly rooted in Christ, who said:

> "In very truth I tell you, unless a grain of wheat falls into the ground and dies, it remains that and nothing more; but if it dies, it bears a rich harvest." (John 12:24)

Culture has taught the students, teachers, and parents of the Saint Monica's community to hide weakness, seek distraction, stay busy, never fall silent or still, and never talk about death, much less think about it. How, then, could anyone from Saint Monica's possibly choose to follow someone like Jesus, who embraced both suffering and death? Given the prevailing culture, such a choice would require a lot of courage.

1
"Laden am I with useless treasure, as with music that has lost its potency for ever. Reveal Thyself to me, O Lord; for all things are hard to one who has lost touch with God" (Antoine de Saint-Exupéry). Think of a time you have felt out of touch with God. Are all things more difficult when you are in that state? Respond in writing.

Saint Monica's culture is probably much like your culture. Putting faith in Jesus Christ requires an act of courage. Christians follow someone who walked willingly into death, because that someone alone knows the way back from the grave! A culture can evade, distort, and deny its own mortality. Still, a person can choose to move toward death with hope, with Jesus Christ, with faith in God's promise: "'I am with you always; yes, to the end of time'" (Matthew 28:20).

You are reading a book about death. As your own feelings about this subject begin to surface, you might feel confused and anxious. The story of the storm at night can help. Why? Because the night was transformed, and with that transformation came an important discovery.

A Night of Terror and Awe

Begin by recalling that something extraordinary happened the night of the storm, a thing both terrifying and wondrous. Recall, too, that the mere memory of this exceptional night calmed someone as intense as Father George.

The night had begun simply enough. Some friends had boarded a boat and set out together on a lake. Jesus was one of the people on board. Soon after setting out, he fell asleep. Fatigue was not unusual for Jesus, as he was mobbed daily by huge crowds of people: some curious, some excited, some wounded, some aching and sobbing, some grieving, some dying. All who pursued Jesus hungered for something from him.

> The night was transformed, and with it came an important discovery.

Such crowds inevitably included those who were hungering for his destruction and death—you can imagine how this alone would tire a person!

But the disciples in the boat were not focused on Jesus' exhaustion. Something else had caught their attention. Without warning, a violent windstorm had risen up over the lake. Being in a small craft in a fierce storm can be terrifying. The storm, sudden and brutal, swamped the boat. Waves were breaking right over the sides. Their fragile vessel, quickly overwhelmed by the force of the wind and the waves, was going down. Incredibly, Jesus' sleep was not disturbed by the storm.

It was something else that caused him to awaken.

The disciples, fearing they would perish, rushed to Jesus and woke him, saying, "Save us Lord, we are lost!" They were looking straight into the face of death as if they were utterly alone; they were experiencing true terror. What Jesus' friends hoped he would do is unknown to us. But they were likely surprised by his first words upon waking up.

He asked them a question: "Why are you so terrified, you of little faith?" Now this might seem to be a ridiculous question in the midst of a storm's fury, but Jesus asked it anyway. He didn't wait for an answer, though. Instead, he got up and spoke to the waves. At once, the wind and the sea died down. Suddenly, all was dead calm.

Astonished, the disciples had a question of their own: "Who is it that wind and sea obey?"

Experiencing terror in the face of a sudden storm was a natural human reaction, one that Jesus understood. But Jesus was disappointed with the disciples' lack of faith in the midst of their fear. He knew that with stronger faith, their terror—though real—would not have overwhelmed them.

The problem was that the disciples were looking right into the heart of that storm without faith, which means they were looking right into the face of death—without faith. To contemplate death in this way can be disturbing and shattering. The storm had caused the disciples' terror. Their facing that storm with so little faith had caused a much deeper anguish. No wonder they panicked. Jesus cared not only because they were terrified by the storm, but because of the deeper anguish they were suffering. Jesus' concern for the disciples had to do not only with the high winds and raging seas, the outer storm, but also with their emotional turmoil, the inner storm. He wanted those he loved to be able to see with the eyes of faith—to see life in the face of death.

What sort of person is able to see the hidden anguish of the soul?

What sort of person knows the way back from the grave?

2
Write a poem or paragraph responding to this question: *What sort of person do wind and sea obey?*

Truth Rooted in Love

It is Jesus Christ who rises up in the middle of the night, addressing the waves and subduing them. As he takes charge of the storm, people like the disciples, like Father George, like us can become calm. When Jesus comes, the storm—both within and without—dies down. Stunned by unexpected peace, we discover the power of faith and the power of God. One who wants to follow Christ knows that suffering is meant to be embraced, and lived intimately with the God who loves and shapes us in the very midst of suffering.

At the height of our own troubles, Jesus might well ask us, "Why are you so terrified, you of little faith?" His concern about our lack of faith would not be an expression of ridicule. It would be an expression of love. God realizes that fear is part of life. God wants to help us with our fears. In all our storms, both those within and those without, God works to transform fear with the gift of faith. Strengthened by faith, we need not be dismayed by the cultural clamor that says, "Don't talk about death" and "Never grow old, never fall silent or still." Christians need not fear truth. In fact, truth alone can free us from fear.

To Seek as We Struggle

Whatever you are feeling as you continue this study of death—whether it be curiosity, fear, anxiety, doubt, anger, guilt, resentment, powerlessness, confusion, or something else—begin by being reassured. Jesus saved his friends from their distress even though, at the critical moment, they lost faith.

God does not ask us to have unshakable faith—that's a human impossibility. But remember what the disciples did when their faith was shaken: they ran to get Jesus. All we are asked to do is to seek God as we struggle to believe.

3
Write an essay agreeing or disagreeing with the following statement: Wanting to believe is the beginning of believing.

Death and Life Go Together

Death is real. Death is inescapable. Christians find hope in God, the one who transforms all things, even the radical separation of body and spirit that comes about at the moment of death. None of us now reading this book has yet undergone that radical separation, as we are still alive.

Yet, each of us—even the youngest of us—has already experienced some aspects of both death and resurrection. Think of a newborn child who has just lost the safe, warm world of the womb; this loss is a kind of death. But that child is born into a much larger world, a world of light, of new tastes and sounds, a world of far greater possibilities than any the womb could ever offer.

Everyday Transformations

Death and dying are part of each day. And each day, God goes about the work of transforming things. Let's look at a few examples.

The sun over Saint Monica's goes down at the end of each day. Each night, darkness descends; the stars come out, and stillness blankets the earth. And then dawn comes, bringing with it the quiet rising of another day's sun.

Each year, Saint Monica's is buried by the snow, lashed by the icy winds of winter. But every spring, things turn green again and the warmth returns.

Red poppies are planted outside the front doors of the school. They bloom tall and gorgeous all summer long. Then slowly their petals open so wide they begin to fall off. Before school starts again, their color fades. The plants become yellow and tired looking. Where there was once a bright red bloom, now there is nothing but a small gray hub, an unattractive orb on top of a dry yellow stem. But this ugly, hard gray hub is a remarkable storehouse, a small, carefully crafted package of tiny poppy seeds. The ugly gray hub contains an entire field of next year's red poppies.

The staff and students at Saint Monica's have experienced aspects of dying and rising. Sarah experienced loss early in life when her mother left. But that loss made her more aware of her hunger for love. That loss made her more open to the love she found with her grandmother.

Remember Keisha and Jerome? When last we heard of them, they had stopped speaking to each other. Keisha felt crushed by Jerome's failure to understand her. Jerome felt as if their relationship and their future had been shattered. Keisha felt afraid to trust him again. In their breakup, they experienced a kind of death.

However, the night Keisha sat cuddling her black kitten, reading the poem about Jesus' dying thoughts, she decided to try again. It took her another day to summon up the courage to phone Jerome. Jerome, too, was wanting to try again. "Jerome, I'm sorry," she started. That's all Jerome needed to hear: "I'm sorry too. I didn't mean to hurt you. I really didn't." That was the beginning of their getting back together again. Both felt inwardly relieved to know that a breakdown in a relationship need not mean the relationship is over forever.

Daily Living and Daily Dying

Every human life is filled with ups and downs, deaths and resurrections. Take a moment to see if that is true of your own life. In the last twenty-four hours, can you recall a moment of "dying," in nature, in yourself, or in a relationship? Can you recall a moment of "rising"? Experiences of dying and rising happen all the time. In fact, it's unlikely that any person could go a full day with absolutely no experiences of dying or rising.

> Every human life is filled with ups and downs, deaths and resurrections.

If you've ever been hurt by a friend, you've experienced a kind of death. If you've ever apologized to someone you've hurt, you already know a little bit about resurrection. The capacity to suffer becomes the capacity to love. A disagreement doesn't have to mean the end of a relationship, and a loss doesn't have to mean you'll never be happy again. We learn something each time we rise up from the little deaths we go through every day. We are transformed by our dying and our rising.

With faith, we can learn that death and grief are not the end of the story. If we see with the eyes of faith, we can realize that death leads us to life, to new life, to a kind of joy that shall not be taken from us. Jesus labored every day of his ministry to make this truth known to his disciples. In Saint John's Gospel, Jesus promised, "'So you have pain now; but I will see you again, and your hearts will rejoice, and no one will take your joy from you'" (John 16:22). Christian hope is built on this promise.

We Need Our Questions

All of life's griefs and deaths, big and small, touch us, offering to challenge and transform us. Dying and grieving are rich with intense contrasts: sadness, love, rage, guilt, confusion, fear, powerlessness, hope. Father George suffered because of his dad's illness. However, suffering deepened his love for his father, taught him to cry, and gave him a more compassionate heart. Suffering and grieving brought Father George other gifts as well, gifts he has yet to discover. Such is the nature of grief.

Grief uncovers questions long hidden in secret places. Why must I be betrayed by my best friend? Why do I so often fail? How can I believe in a God of love when God allows someone I love to be killed in a car accident? Why didn't God intervene to save the life of my friend? Why did

God make me with a capacity for so much suffering? Why did God create me for love, then place me in a world that will surely force me to face the loss of all that I most cherish? If God has promised that my dead friend will be raised to new life, why doesn't God just come right out and say that in plain and simple language? Why am I filled with doubt and uncertainty? Why do I feel so alone with this? Is there a God at all?

We need not fear raising up our secret, most troubling questions. We need our questions. They become friends to us, friends leading us into the rich and mysterious depths of our own self.

We Need Our Emotions, Even the Painful Ones

Our questions and our emotions rise up together; we need both. Anger teaches us to locate our hurts and to recognize our values. Keisha and Jerome were angry with each other when their relationship faltered. But anger led them to understand their hurts a little better, to see what had gone wrong.

Jerome felt guilty for what he had done to Keisha. The guilt was awful, but it led him to see that he really cared about Keisha and didn't want to hurt her. Both learned that love makes us more vulnerable and opens us to getting hurt. But they also learned that forgiving each other after a fight makes a relationship stronger.

> We need not fear raising our secret, most troubling questions.

Hurt and loss lead us to struggle and to search. Emotions are gifts from God; they are tools of tremendous value. Emotions are not to be buried or shunned, but to be felt and used in the struggling and in the searching. We need them. Used wisely, our emotions can help lead us to the best that life has to offer.

Our emotions and our questions are particularly indispensable when death strikes.

Throughout your study of death and dying, remember that God's love and power are at work in our midst. God leads us through the storm into the calm. God is constantly at work to transform us so that in sorrow, we learn to become vulnerable; in anguish, we learn to be comforted; in grief, we learn to move into the depths of love; in fear and questioning, we begin to discover the depth of real faith.

God's radical transformation of fear into faith and despair into hope is a gift, a grace. And God's gifts do not come to an end. With God, life itself becomes grace upon grace. Therefore, we can be confident and at peace, even when death becomes our subject.

With Great Care, We Turn Inward

Father George keeps the following prayer in the front of his engagement calendar. Sometimes he's in a good mood when he reads it; sometimes he reads it when he's angry, sad, or lonely. No matter how he's feeling when he reads it, though, he entrusts his living and his dying into God's hands.

God,
forgive me
when I abandon you.
I am so fragile, so fearing, so hurting, and so doubting.
Deep down, I know that my death is real and inescapable.
Deep down, my questions have no answers.

I am in your hands.
Raise up my questions with gentleness.
Make me courageous, hopeful, and wise.
Stay in my heart.

O Death,
teach me the wild and rich graces brought you
by Jesus Christ.
Teach me your secrets, your depths,
the potential given you by the One who risked everything
for love.

O Christ,
I am yours.
You surrendered yourself into death.
I surrender myself into you.
Be with me when I grieve.
Be with me when I die.
O my soul, stay with your God.

Dearest Christ, teach me love.

The Christian Voice

When the world says, "Just pretend you'll never die," Christians choose instead to seek the truth. We know it is not we who spun the stars into orbit, nor we who stoked the first great fire, the burning sun. In fact, we ourselves cannot make one single thing out of nothing. But that's okay because God is with us. Our job is to discover, shape, and exult in all that God has created for us, to enter with God into our living, dying, and rising.

4
For you, what does it mean to entrust your living, dying, and rising into God's hands? Compose your own prayer of trust.

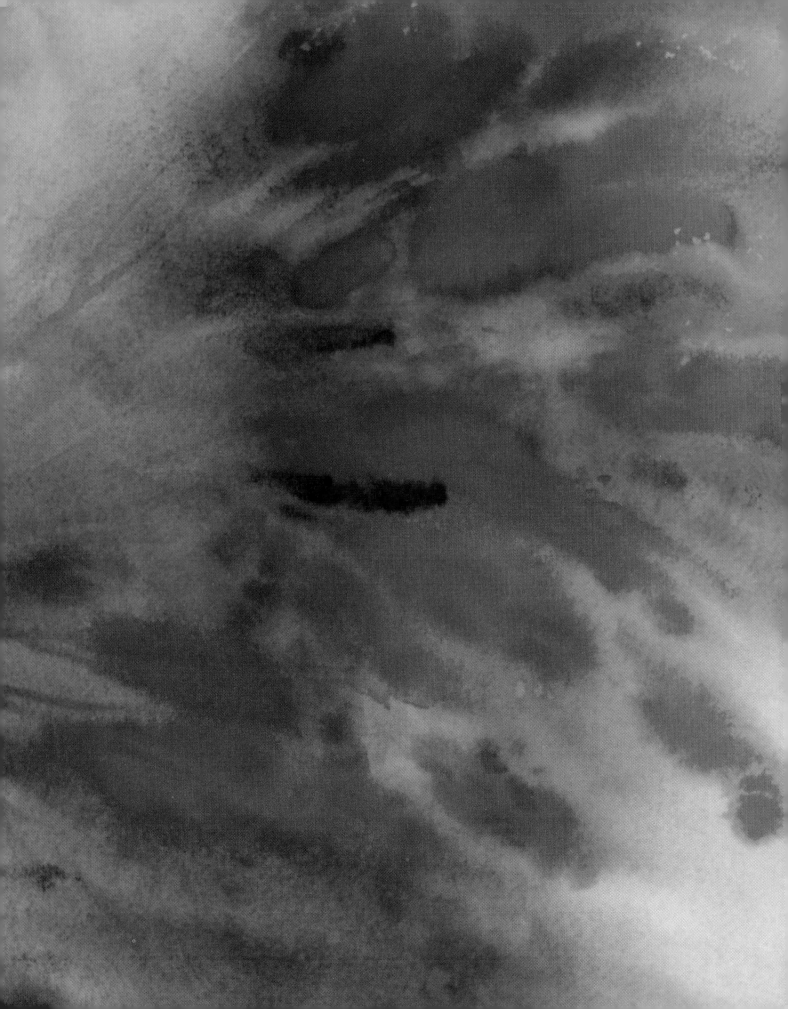

4 A Roman Catholic Funeral

I do not believe that sheer suffering teaches. If suffering alone taught, all the world would be wise, since everyone suffers. To suffering must be added mourning, understanding, patience, love, openness and willingness to remain vulnerable.

—Anne Morrow Lindbergh

Procession

"The grace and peace of God our Father and the Lord Jesus Christ be with you." Sarah is weeping. She stands just inside the door of Saint Luke's Church with her boyfriend, Mike, her father, her brother, relatives, and friends. The coffin containing the body of Sarah's grandmother, Martha Spencer, is being sprinkled with holy water. Her funeral has begun.

Father Jim reminds those present that the first time this body was sprinkled with holy water, Martha was an infant: "In the waters of Baptism, Martha died with Christ and rose with him to new life. May she now share with him eternal glory."

At Baptism, Martha, an infant dressed in white, was welcomed into the church and clothed with a new and vital garment: the life of Christ. Decades later, despite a yearlong battle with cancer, Martha's inner vitality had been evident until the day she died; she was only fifty-nine years old.

Sarah imagines the lighting of candles for her grandmother's christening. God's gift of life must have been easy to see and wonderful to celebrate that day. Today nothing is easy, and Sarah does not feel like celebrating.

A Heavy Pall

Everyone is sad and motionless now. Sarah finds it almost impossible to believe that there can be life after death. She has stopped trusting God. Earlier, she was puzzled to hear her uncle referring to the funeral as the Mass of the Resurrection. With gloom all around, and her grandmother gone, Sarah cannot see how this service has anything much to do with resurrection.

Today there are no smiling faces, no rosy-cheeked babies dressed in white. Instead, there is a coffin draped with white velvet; the baptismal garment has become a heavy pall. It hurts so much that Sarah has to look away.

Sarah diverts her thoughts to the gold ring that was her grandmother's, the ring Sarah lost in art class. Sarah was so relieved the day it was found. Now she lightly caresses the ring. It comforts her to touch what remains of the tiny roses carved all around it.

Father Jim now proclaims God's promise: "Those we love will live forever." Sarah would prefer to scream than to proclaim some ridiculous hope about eternal life.

Someone Has Gone Before Us

Sarah finds herself in a procession moving up the main aisle of the church. She and the others are following the dead. And Sarah aches, knowing that later they will be following the dead all the way to the gravesite.

Sarah finds some comfort in the tall white candle flaming at the head of the procession, just behind the cross. Luckily she is able to see this one candle over the top of Uncle Philip's head. Sarah is calmed a little by following that flame, as if it were a torch pulling her through a dark tunnel.

The calming effect of the light at the head of this funeral procession is no accident. The church uses light to symbolize hope, strength, and love. Light reminds us of the unseen Someone at the head of this pilgrimage, Christ himself. We are never alone at a funeral. Christ is the unseen source of the hope, strength, and love we need in our grief. It is he who has already gone before us, all the way to the grave. It is he who has returned from the grave, alive.

Christ has come back to take us with him, through our own grieving and dying, into a new life we can barely imagine. The cross, which precedes the candle, tells the story of his journey—and ours. The candle proclaims his promise:

1
A few decades ago it was customary to drape the coffin with a black or dark purple pall. In that era, even the priest was vested in black. These days the church's funeral vestments are white, the symbol of resurrection. Is this change consistent with the way you think about death? Write your answer in a paragraph.

Christ is the unseen source of the hope, strength, and love we need in our grief.

"I am the light of the world;
anyone who follows me will not be walking in the dark,
but will have the light of life."

(John 8:12)

Though he is unseen, Jesus Christ is leading this woman whose body is now being borne in a casket. He is also leading Sarah, although it doesn't feel that way to her. And when Sarah reaches the grave, Christ will be standing beside her. The voice of the mourning community will proclaim that Martha Spencer's life is not ended, but united now with Christ.

The entrance procession is accompanied by a song of praise, a profound expression of faith in Christ's victory over death. Sarah hears the voices of the people singing, "Be not afraid, I go before you always." But Sarah is afraid. She is not singing.

The Roman Catholic funeral is an expression of grief and hope. In the funeral Mass, it is not only the casket that is carried but the mourners as well. All are carried by the One who poured out both tears and blood. Each of us will pass through the inevitable aching of a funeral, and will stand in sadness at the graveside of someone we love. But no one stands alone. And Sarah has not been abandoned by God.

The people at Martha's funeral continue the entrance song: "If you stand before the power of hell and death is at your side, know that I am with you through it all." What is impossible for us alone becomes possible with God. Despite her despair, the truth is that in Christ, Sarah is still together with her grandmother. The two are united in the Spirit.

They Laughed at Him

As the entrance procession slowly continues, with the light and the cross at its head, Sarah's mind goes back to last semester's religion class with Ms. Shields. They were studying a Gospel story about death. A man, going out of his mind because his twelve-year-old daughter was dying, ran out to get Jesus. But Jesus was busy curing somebody else. The man's daughter died.

Sarah could imagine that father's sense of injustice: "Why should someone else have been cured instead of my daughter? If only Jesus could have saved her." Sarah thinks to herself: "If only we were not walking up this aisle in Grandma's funeral procession. At age fifty-nine, she was too young to die. If only God could have kept Mom and Dad from breaking up."

As the funeral procession nears the altar, the people are still singing the opening song of praise and victory, the air is still filled with the words of Jesus: "Be not afraid." Sarah remembers more of the story. Jesus told the anguished father not to be afraid, that his daughter would be well again. Jesus told the man to have faith.

Sarah thinks it's impossible to have faith at a funeral. She is inwardly fuming: "That father knew it was stupid to think that a dead person could rise. I bet he'd like to have blasted Jesus: 'Why do you insult and torture me with empty words about faith when my daughter is dead?'" Sarah has no kind thoughts for the God who allowed her grandmother to develop cancer, to suffer horribly, and then to die.

Sarah cannot seem to get this Gospel story out of her head. Jesus went to the young girl's house. Sarah had always thought his first words to the mourners were so stupid. He told them that the girl was not dead, just sleeping. Sarah figures they must have thought Jesus was out of his mind.

Sarah vividly recalls the family's reaction to Jesus. They laughed at him. How insane they must have thought him! Sarah's thoughts suddenly shift back to the present. She finds the words of the opening song quite annoying: "If you pass through raging waters in the sea, you shall not drown."

2
"If only . . ." is a common lament of those who have suffered a loss. We have a natural urge to undo what has been done, to regain what has been lost. With that lament comes a sense of powerlessness—we cannot change what has happened. Write a poem or a page-long essay about an experience in which you heard yourself saying, "If only . . ."

"Why are we singing songs of praise," she wonders, "when my grandma is dead?" In the Gospel story, the people standing around the girl's deathbed laughed at Jesus. If Sarah could laugh right now, she'd laugh right in God's face.

But Sarah remembers how the story ends: Jesus told the dead girl to get up. And she did. Sarah finds herself thinking: "I wish I could believe that Grandma will somehow live on after death. I wish I could believe I wasn't going to die of this pain. Will this dumb procession never come to an end?"

The Lord Has Heard

It is with relief that Sarah finally sinks into the cold comfort of the front pew. More prayers have been said, but she has not heard them. Suddenly she is aware of Mike. He's holding her hand, the hand bearing the gold ring. She watches as the casket is wheeled in front of a candle that must be three feet tall. This is the Easter candle, a symbol of Christ's victory over death.

As Sarah watches her older brother walk slowly up to the lectern, she's glad she said she couldn't do a reading. She knew her knees would have been shaking, and she probably would have been unable to speak.

Greg's voice is steady as he reads from Isaiah:

> "The Lord GOD will wipe away
>   the tears
> from every face."
>
> (25:8)

Over the past year, Sarah often wished she could wipe away her grandmother's tears. Greg returns to his seat. Not realizing what she is doing, Sarah begins to picture Jesus drying the tears on her grandmother's face; that picture makes her feel good.

Sarah hears more singing. This time, it's a solo, a single, clear voice filling the church. It's Uncle Philip singing the psalm:

"I was sure I should be swept away;
my distress was bitter.

.   .   .   .

I shall lift up the cup of salvation
and call on the LORD by name."

(Psalm 116:10–13)

Sarah is amazed at how that one single voice echoes, how it seems so effortlessly carried through the whole church.

In the silence that follows the clear, pure voice of the psalm, Sarah hears the people's response:

"I love the LORD, for he has heard me
and listened to my prayer."

(Psalm 116:1)

The gold ring of tiny carved roses feels so secure on her finger, her hand so warm and protected inside Mike's. Sarah finds it a little easier to breathe now. She wonders what it means to lift up the cup of salvation.

Even Jesus Wept

"He cried out in a loud voice, 'Lazarus, come out!'" (John 11:43). Sarah is embarrassed to realize she did not hear a single word of the entire second reading. It's Father Jim's voice she is hearing now, as he reads the Gospel. Fortunately, she knows the story of Lazarus. Lazarus, a close friend of Jesus', died while Jesus was in another town. It had always amazed Sarah that Jesus actually cried when he heard of Lazarus's death. She could never understand how Jesus could be that upset if he knew he was just about to raise Lazarus from the grave.

Sarah tunes in again to Father Jim's voice: "The dead man came out, tied hand and foot with burial bands, and his face was wrapped in a cloth. So Jesus said to them, 'Untie him and let him go'" (John 11:44). Sarah nearly gasps out loud. What had felt like heavy chains around her chest are suddenly gone. She doesn't hear a single word of the homily. But now she is leaning back, and she's breathing freely, without the slightest effort.

For the first time, she notices the large bouquets of flowers all around the altar. Red roses are arranged with tall white lilies and a lot of greenery. To Sarah, the bouquets look stiff and unnatural. She wishes that whoever arranged the flowers had not forced so many into each vase. She even thinks that the flowers might look more comfortable if they had not been made to stand up so straight and be so evenly spaced.

3
Jesus was as human as Sarah is human. At the grave of Lazarus, Jesus suffered. But he had faith that Lazarus would be raised, and he acted on that faith. Have you ever acted on such faith?

She can't help realizing how much better she feels to be breathing freely again.

During the prayers of intercession, there is a pause for private petitions. Not having intended to trust God enough to ask for anything, Sarah is surprised to find her own silent plea pouring out of her: "Help me, God. Help me, God. Help me, God."

4
Which of these statements do you agree with?
- Asking God for help is a tremendous act of faith.
- Asking God for help is an act of despair.
Give your reasons in a paragraph.

Take This, and Drink

The congregation, having been fed by God's word in the first part of the funeral Mass, turn next to God's banquet table, the table of the Eucharist, the table at which Jesus ate and drank just before he died. They move toward that mysterious meal in which Jesus offered them food and drink from his own hands, begging them: "Take this, all of you . . . this is my body. . . . This is the cup of my blood."

The Cup of Salvation

Sarah thinks that the cup Jesus held out to his friends might be the same as the cup of salvation her uncle was singing about in the psalm. At the Last Supper, the Apostles drank from the cup Jesus offered. It amazed Sarah that they had freely lifted that cup to their own lips. She had never thought too much about it before, but now she wonders how the Apostles felt when they drank from the cup Jesus held out to them as the cup of his own blood.

She herself had often drunk from the cup at Communion, and it hadn't meant much to her. But today, having experienced her grandmother's pain and death, Sarah has a better understanding of what it means for blood to be poured out. Today, if she chooses to drink from the cup, it will require courage never before demanded of her.

Sarah is watching as Father Jim picks up the cup and says: "When supper was ended, he took the cup. Again he gave you thanks and praise, gave the cup to his disciples and said: 'Take this, all of you, and drink from it.'" The cup is in Father Jim's hands, lifted high above his head. She wonders if he finds it difficult to lift it up so high like that.

Thy Will Be Done

Sarah is aware now that everyone has stood up. The whole church seems motionless and quiet, except for the collective

voice singing, "Thy kingdom come, thy will be done, on earth as it is in heaven."

"What is 'thy will'?" Sarah wonders. "O God, what could you possibly want from me? In all this pain and hurting, where could you be leading me? What will happen to me if I drink the blood of Christ today? Why must this ring be on my finger now when I wish so much that it had never left Grandma's hand?"

Sarah remembers how impressed she always was watching her grandmother's skillful hands at the computer keyboard. She thinks to herself: "Grandma had been doing useful work; couldn't God see that the world needed her? Couldn't God see that I still needed my grandmother? But then, why should God see any of that?" God certainly didn't seem to notice Sarah's hurt so many years ago when her mother moved out.

Sarah would later come to learn that the grieving process is more difficult when there have been earlier, unresolved losses. Sarah's hurt over her mother's abandonment had been repressed. Sarah's father never talked about it. Nor did her grandmother; she was angry with Sarah's mother for leaving the family. Sarah's grief over this experience did not come to the surface until now, at her grandmother's death.

Sometimes people can bury unresolved grief for ten years, twenty years—even a lifetime. When grief is buried, a part of the self is buried along with it. One of Sarah's tasks, as she continues to mature, will be to fully uncover and deal with that grief.

Hugging and Kissing in Church

"Lord Jesus Christ, you said to your Apostles, 'I leave you peace, my peace I give you.'" Sarah's father holds her hand and kisses her. She hugs her aunt, her brother, and her friends. The Sign of Peace has never before felt like this. And the people begin singing again, "Peace is flowing like a river . . . setting all the captives free."

Sarah knows what it means to be captive; she knows she is locked inside her own sadness. She knows her grandmother was a captive—a skilled and gifted woman who rapidly lost the ability to sit up at her own computer, a woman captured by untreatable cancer. Sarah knows that captives are those who have lost their freedom.

Peace is flowing like a river. Martha Spencer is now free of her cancer. Sarah's father is free from dreading the day of his mother's death. Sarah's older brother, Greg, who never touches anyone, is putting his arms around everyone he can reach. To her utter amazement, she watches as her father reaches over to shake hands warmly with Mike. Sarah's father had always seemed to look down on Mike. She thought her father hated Mike.

Peace is flowing like a river.

Years later Sarah would realize that having lost his wife, her father could not bear the thought of losing his daughter as well. Sarah would begin to understand her father's ambivalence. He pushed her away whenever she tried to get close to him, yet he guarded her as his own property when Mike came on the scene. Her father could bear neither intimacy nor loss; he had learned neither to love nor to grieve.

Even without this understanding, Sarah is stunned to see Mike and her father shaking hands. As Mike turns back to Sarah, she sees a kind of smile she has never before seen on his face. Mike looks like someone who has just received a bouquet of flowers or, perhaps, a standing ovation. For just a moment, Sarah's thoughts are not thoughts of death.

Sarah is still breathing freely. And she's crying as they sing, "Peace is flowing like a river, flowing out of you and me." For the first time since she sat down in the front pew,

Sarah allows herself to look at the coffin again. She is hoping her grandmother can somehow hear the singing. Sarah wonders whether to drink from the cup at Communion time, whether she will be able to "lift up the cup of salvation."

Have Mercy on Us

"Lamb of God, you take away the sins of the world: have mercy on us. . . . Have mercy on us. . . . Grant us peace."

"Happy are those who are called to his supper."

"Only say the word and I shall be healed."

A baby is crying. It's Uncle Philip and Aunt Tish's son, Corey. And Corey is absolutely wailing. Inside, Sarah herself is almost wailing: "Have mercy on me, God. I want to be healed."

As Communion is distributed, people begin getting up and filing past the casket. They're singing another song now: "Amazing grace, how sweet the sound that saved a wretch like me. I once was lost, but now I'm found; was blind, but now I see." It hurts so much for Sarah to walk past the coffin, but doing so will help her to accept her loss.

Still stunned by her father's reaching out to Mike, Sarah feels a lump in her throat. She watches as her father takes

Communion from the cup. She thinks of Jesus, the one who risked everything for love. What will happen to her today if his blood runs through her veins? Sarah takes the Host. Her mouth is dry from crying. She fears she will not be able to swallow. She stands in front of the cup. She takes a deep breath. With visions of her father's extended hand and Mike's smile, Sarah tilts the gold chalice toward her lips. She takes the tiniest sip. As she walks back to her place in the front row, she feels a rush of warmth.

Sinking back into the front pew again, she is surprised to find that she swallows the Host easily. "God, I am still scared and still sad, but I want to ask you to do something. Lift up my grandma the way they talked about lifting up the cup in the psalm. God, lift up my grandma."

To Gather Again in Joy

Father Jim begins the rite of commendation and farewell, the final prayers over the casket. Sarah begins to ache again. He's talking about the final farewell, the final parting that must now come. She almost wishes she could hear Corey screaming again, because she knows that she herself must remain silent, that she herself must not cry out.

For a moment, an unfamiliar scent distracts Sarah from the urge to scream. It is incense, an ancient substance used since the earliest times of the church. Perfumed smoke rises when incense is burned. The rising incense is like the community's prayer rising up to God.

The rising incense is like the community's prayer rising up to God.

Sarah watches smoke rise over the coffin. It curls upward into the air. Incense is a sign of respect to the body of the dead person. The human body is honored as a temple of the Spirit, a flesh-and-blood house in which humanity and divinity meet. Martha Spencer's body is treated with the utmost reverence. In this body she lived, and Christ lived in her.

Father Jim is talking about the sadness. He says that although this congregation will go away in sorrow, they will be gathered together again in the Kingdom's joy. The faith and hope of the church is that one day they will see Martha again, alive. This certainly is Sarah's deepest hope. Sarah thinks once more about the parents of the little girl raised to life by Jesus. She wishes so much for that mother and father to join their hope with hers.

Father Jim completes the prayer: "Into your hands, Father of mercies, we commend our sister Martha, in the sure and certain hope that together with all who have died in Christ, she will rise with him on the last day."

A New Creation

Once again, Sarah finds herself following the casket. They are taking her grandmother's body to the gravesite. Again she can see the candle flame at the head of the procession, just behind the cross. That helps.

However, this closing procession is not the same as the entrance procession, at least not for Sarah. As they had formed a line behind the casket for the entrance procession, Sarah thought that the gravesite was to be the final step in the journey. She has now begun to realize that the final destination is far beyond the gravesite. The sounds of the closing song are starting to fill the church: "My life flows on in endless song; above earth's lamentation. I hear the real though far-off hymn that hails a new creation. . . . How can I keep from singing?"

Sarah, her grandmother, her family, and her friends are pilgrims making their way to God's Kingdom. The graveyard is part of their long journey, but not their final destiny.

Outpouring

The procession reaches the doors of the church. This somber crowd, having held in its tears, its screams, its rage, and its cries for the full length of the funeral, now pours out onto the street. With unexpected relief, talk and laughter pour out of the people, creating such a din that Sarah can just barely hear the fading words of the closing song: "No storm can shake my inmost calm, while to that Rock I'm clinging. Since Love is Lord of heaven and earth, how can I keep from singing?"

As the casket is lifted into the hearse, Sarah's father is standing beside her. Something has changed. Words are pouring out of him. He's talking to her—not with a newspaper in one hand or with a glance away from the TV set, but with his full attention. Sarah and her father have so rarely spoken to each other over the past few years. Mike's presence had strained their relationship even further. Yet, at this moment, her father's gaze feels unbelievably gentle.

In all probability, Sarah will not remember the words her father is saying to her right now. What she will remember is the warmth in his eyes, the warmth on her face.

The church doors are closing, and the driver has started the engine of the long black hearse. Sarah has always hated the word *hearse*. She hates the idea of the coffin going into a dark car. Floating above the crowd and finding its way into Sarah's soul is the final faint sound of her grandmother's

5
Laughter is a gift from God. At funerals, laughter can be a form of emotional release, a way of lightening the load and taking a break from the labor of grief. The gift of laughter becomes destructive, though, when it is used to deny sorrow and bury pain. Write a description of a time when you experienced laughter as either healthy release or destructive denial.

funeral Mass: "What though the darkness 'round me close, songs in the night it giveth."

Pilgrims, Still

It feels good to be off her feet again, sitting against the door in the backseat of Uncle Philip's car. This is the first chance Mike has had to speak to her since before the funeral started. He is talking about her father and the way they shook hands during the Sign of Peace. He's so excited about the possibility of being accepted by Mr. Spencer that he's actually dreaming of one day marrying Sarah.

But Sarah is thinking about the graveyard. As Uncle Philip drives and Aunt Tish sits beside him, Corey sleeps in the car seat between Sarah and Mike. Sarah wishes he were awake. It would help to see his blue eyes right now. It would help to play with him, even just a little. But Corey continues to sleep. Over her ring finger, Sarah gently curls the little boy's tiny fingers.

The Open Gates

The funeral cortege is nearing the big black iron gates at the cemetery entrance. The gates are open. They pass through.

And Sarah feels herself sink. No sounds of song reach her now. All that she feels is a chilling emptiness. She dreads seeing the grave. She dreads arriving there. With the chill comes a new kind of ache. Sarah sinks even lower.

She is remembering the many nights last fall when she left the house in the early evening and did not return until late. She knew her grandmother would wait up all night long, if need be, to see Sarah come through the door. But being with Mike had been great. Mike had been all Sarah could think about. And Sarah had often stayed out late.

Guilt settles over her like the heavy branches of the evergreens leaning on the top of the car as it comes to a stop. Even one phrase of "Be Not Afraid" would feel like heaven. But no music comes. Sarah asks Aunt Tish if she can carry the sleeping baby. Gratefully, Sarah pulls Corey into her arms.

She approaches the grave. Her grandmother's casket has been placed over it. The sun is bright, and the sky blue. She would have preferred a cold, heavy downpour and a dark sky. In her guilt, she feels that this is what she deserves. With one hand, she rearranges Corey's bonnet so that it covers his ears.

"I'm sorry, I'm so sorry. Can you ever forgive me?" Sarah's father is speaking to her. Guilt has descended on him too. All these years, he has been pushing Sarah away, yet trying to keep her from Mike. Finally, he is able to apologize. As he does, Sarah feels the warmth of the sun. And she's breathing again. A sigh of relief has come from somewhere inside her. She thinks that maybe she will not die of her guilt. She might live through it after all.

The rite of committal is deliberately stark and simple; it underscores the radical separation between body and soul.

> ## "Lord Jesus, you wept at the grave of Lazarus; comfort us."

Yet it also expresses one true hope: that we shall rise again. Father Jim is praying aloud: "Because God has chosen to call our sister Martha from this life to himself, we commit her body to the earth. . . . But the Lord Jesus Christ will change our mortal bodies to be like his in glory, for he is risen. Lord Jesus, you wept at the grave of Lazarus, your friend; comfort us now in our sorrow." Father Jim stretches out his hands over the whole crowd, "Merciful God, you know the anguish of the sorrowful, hear your people who cry out to you in their need."

The Goodness of the Lord

Still holding Corey, Sarah reaches to pick up a rose. She chooses a white one. She places her rose gently on the coffin. Sarah can't help wishing that the coffin could be completely covered with roses of all colors—orange, yellow, pink, white, red. The idea that the coffin will later be buried with earth is scary, but somehow soothing too. Even the dark earth is a covering, like a huge, rich blanket of warm protection.

It had never occurred to Sarah that anyone could sing in a graveyard. There is no organ out here. But again, the sounds of song reach into her soul. Somehow this singing, at this moment, even with no accompaniment, is better than an entire orchestra. The voices of the people fill the emptiness of the graveyard, falling softly on all present. They keep repeating a single line, "Say to the Lord: 'My refuge, my Rock in whom I trust.'"

That single line, Sarah sings. With the sound of so many voices, Corey stirs a little in Sarah's arms. She hopes he will wake up.

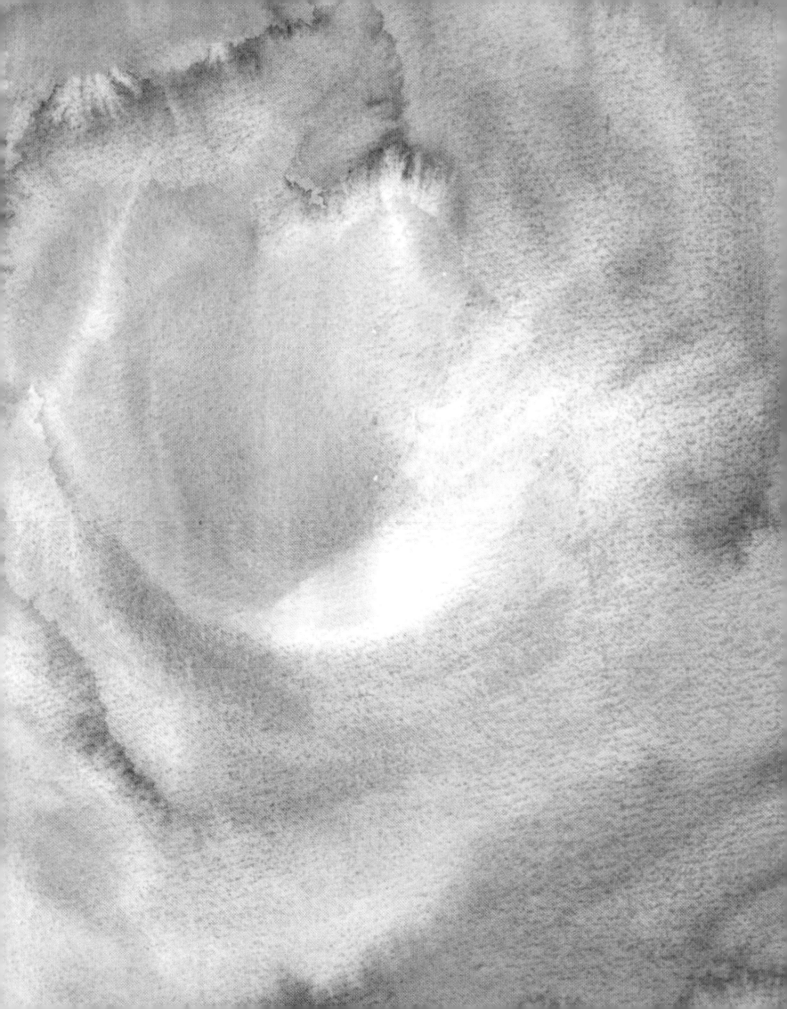

5
Beyond the Horizon

Death is only a horizon; and a horizon is nothing save the limit of our sight.
—Rossiter Worthington Raymond

David's Journey

Veronica Shields had a brother named David. David Shields was built like a football player—all muscle and brawn. At least that's how he appeared on the outside. On the inside, David lived in constant fear, debilitating self-doubt, and silent desperation. David was manic-depressive, meaning that he struggled intensely with various forms of uncontrolled mania alternating with suicidal depression.

In his manic phase, David was on a kind of high. Unfortunately, the manic-depressive version of a high is fraught with danger; mania is a mental disability often characterized by excessive activity and an unreasonably inflated self-image. During a manic high, David might, for example, engage in vigorous activities for days without pausing to rest, then shout angrily at a friend or family member for advising him to slow down and get some sleep.

David's mania was always followed by depression, at times so severe that he contemplated suicide.

One day, several years before she began teaching at Saint Monica's High School, Veronica received a call from the local police department. On that day, in the pale of early morning, David had fallen victim to another kind of misfortune. It happened not long after his twenty-fourth birthday. On a quiet dead-end street, two hooded figures approached silently from behind, then pounced on David and stabbed him. It was his wallet they wanted. They grabbed it, ripped it

open, took the little they found in it, and ran off. There had not been much of a struggle. A short time later, a woman on her way to work found David lying unconscious near the curb in a pool of blood.

David was rushed to a hospital. There, he died. His seemingly unending cycle of tormented extremes was suddenly over. David would suffer no more mania and no more depression.

"O Death, Where Have You Taken the One I Love?"

Veronica Shields had reached the hospital's emergency room shortly after David's death. Aware that other family members would have to drive from out of town, she knew she had to face this moment alone. Veronica was brought to David's bedside by the head nurse. Her initial shock at hearing of her brother's death had begun to wear off. A feeling of anger was about to set in, but as Veronica stood staring at her brother's familiar form, she couldn't help wondering where death had taken David. It was obvious that he was not here in this hospital bed, that he was no longer in this physical body, now lifeless. David was somewhere else now, but where?

For a long time, Veronica remained at David's bedside, motionless. Her chin-length chestnut hair, usually neat and shining, now hung limp and dull. Inert and silent, she ached in her knowledge of David's tortured life. She also ached in her lack of knowledge about where death had led him. Veronica, an intellectual sort of person, often sought knowledge when faced with life's hurts.

Finding the air tinged with the stench of death, Veronica escaped—as she so often did—into her mind. Intellectually, Veronica understood that death is not the end of life but,

1
When someone we love dies, our most urgent questions surface. Typically we ask questions of meaning: What is death? What is life? What happens after death? Who is God? Who are we? Is there really life after death? Reflect on the circumstances in which you have raised your most urgent questions.

rather, its most radical shift. She knew that afterlife is defined in terms of the whole continuum of human existence, the span of life beginning at conception and enduring into eternity. Afterlife is the part of the continuum that follows our existence here on earth.

Life continues after death, yet is changed. Life takes on a new shape. This shape does not involve a physical body and an earthly planet as we know them now. It has to do with the resurrection of body and soul into a kind of existence we have never known before, and cannot fully comprehend now.

At the time of David's death, Veronica Shields was already well versed in Catholic theology. She knew that traditional Roman Catholic teaching speaks of three states of being that follow death: purgatory, heaven, and hell. She realized that David had moved into the afterlife, but she could not know for sure what that would mean for him.

As a child, Veronica had thought of the afterlife as consisting of various chambers. She envisioned purgatory as a kind of waiting room, a pit stop on the way to heaven. She had seen heaven as another kind of chamber, a place of reward and eternal happiness for good people. Images of hell, the third possible destination, had terrified the young Veronica Shields. At that stage of her life, she had understood hell to be a place of endless torture, fiery flame, and gnashing of teeth. She had seen this torture as punishment coming from God.

By the time she was a young adult, Veronica had come to understand that heaven, hell, and purgatory are not necessarily physical places. They are modes of being.

Veronica gingerly stroked David's lifeless hand. She needed to touch the still form lying before her. She closed her eyes. She overheard some of the emergency medical staff, in the hallway, discussing how David had died. They were surprised that he had not survived the assault, such a strong, healthy young man.

God's Love, Without Limits

Veronica understood why David had not survived. She knew he would have welcomed death. She knew that underneath the muscular frame so admired by the world lay a fragile, defenseless heart. For him, life had been a

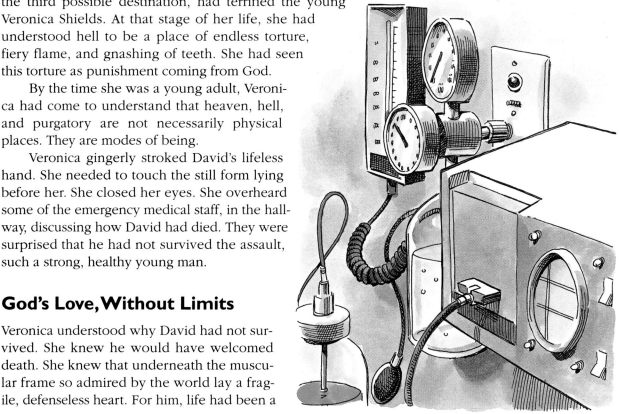

burden. Deep down, Veronica knew that David would not be abandoned into any kind of fiery flame. She no longer thought of God as a punishing power. She had come to know God as Love. In death, this loving God would somehow find David, reaching out to console and heal him.

Veronica's vision of God embracing David matched her mature understanding of heaven. Heaven is the fulfillment of our deepest human longings, the state of pure and unending happiness. It is what Catholic teaching calls the beatific vision—the state in which the human person is in complete union with God. Because heaven surpasses all understanding, the Scriptures speak of it metaphorically: as light, as peace, as a wedding feast, as wine of the Kingdom. Christians believe that shared eternal bliss is God's desire for all people; God wants heaven for us.

Human Freedom Makes the Difference

In life we are free to make choices. Each day, through all our choices, we move toward God and goodness or away from God and goodness. At the moment of death, our history of freely made choices comes to an end. The lifelong exercise of free will culminates in a final stance for or against God, for or against love.

When that final stance is a free choice of love of God, others, and self, the result is entry into heavenly joy. The result of a final stance that rejects God is called hell—a state of permanent self-exclusion from communion with God. Veronica realized that God does not "send" souls to hell. It is God's desire that all will share in the unending joy of heaven. But it is the human choice to reject God that produces a state of permanent separation from God.

God's grace transforms us as much as we are open to it.

Standing by her brother's body, Veronica was sure of two things: God's unending love and David's unending hunger for love.

In both life and death, God's grace transforms us as much as we are open to it. Veronica understood something about human growth. She knew that even though death marks the end of earthly historical and physical development, human progression need not end with death. She could well imagine that in the afterlife, David would continue to need God's purifying graces. David would need God's help in coming to terms with the ways he had resisted love during his lifetime. Veronica prayed that David would open himself completely to God's love, to God's offer of heaven's blissful union.

Theological training had helped Veronica understand purgatory as a kind of spiritual journey, a way of purification, a process by which persons achieve the holiness necessary for entering into the joy of heaven. She found peace in the knowledge that David could be on such a journey.

Judgment Day

Suddenly someone was standing at Veronica's elbow. It was a nurse. In her hand was a watch, the face cracked. The nurse was giving Veronica what remained of David's personal effects, along with some papers in need of signing.

Veronica ached as she took the watch. It was broken, as David's life had been broken. Its two hands were still moving, but they too would eventually stop. Growing into adulthood, Veronica had learned that clocks and calendars pertain only to earthly existence. Such things have no meaning in the next life.

Correspondingly, Veronica's childhood understanding of Judgment Day had also grown and changed. She no longer saw it as the final twenty-four-hour period on our earthly calendar. She no longer pictured a grand assembly in which all persons are systematically directed to their assigned locations in the afterlife.

She came to understand that Judgment is about the coming of Christ. Just as Christ met David at the moment of his death, so too will Christ come to meet all of humanity at the end of the world. In Christ's presence, the truth of every person's relationship with God will be revealed, and all will know the meaning of creation. The Last Judgment, Veronica had learned, is not a literal pronouncement by God, but the culmination and manifestation of the truth.

In the moment of meeting Christ, both at death and at the end of the world, we will see all things as they really are. In the words of Saint Paul: "At present we see only puzzling reflections in a mirror, but one day we shall see face to face. My knowledge now is partial; then it will be whole, like God's knowledge of me" (1 Corinthians 13:12).

A Tear and a Knife

A siren's wail broke into Veronica's consciousness. Veronica looked down at her brother's dead body. She hated to look into his face, yet somehow she had to. She was barely breathing as she moved in closer to him. Slowly, lovingly, her eyes scanned David's features. Then she caught sight of something that shook her. On his cheek was the stain of a single tear. David must have been crying and in pain as he lay dying. Veronica felt a knife pass through her soul.

Her gaze fixed on that lone tear, Veronica moved back into the world of thought. She began to ponder the possibilities of God's grace—human transcendence, the surpassing of former limits. She was imagining David no longer limited by his illness or his own brokenness. She imagined him free, completely free. Another statement from the writings of Saint Paul passed through her mind: "We are groaning inside ourselves, waiting with eagerness for our bodies to be set free. In hope, we already have salvation" (Romans 8:23–24).

A Tear and a Leap of Joy

Floating, as if in a kind of quiet reverie, Veronica pictured David seeing Jesus Christ as he really is. She could imagine her brother, drawn into Christ's love, moving out of death toward God and heaven. As she did, her heart leapt. She

2
Seeing the dead body with our own eyes and touching it with our own hands is part of accepting death's finality. In doing so, we begin the task of saying good-bye to one we have known in the flesh and saying hello to one we shall now know in the spirit. In cases where the body cannot be viewed, grieving can become prolonged and complicated. Given the choice, would you choose to view the body of a loved one, or would you choose not to?

sensed David's spirit being somehow in motion, not arrested as his physical functioning was now arrested. She had always known intellectually that life continues after death; now she knew it more deeply than ever before.

Veronica did not realize it, but she had been standing at her brother's deathbed for more than an hour. A hospital volunteer came over and placed a chair behind her. Gratefully, she sank into its comfort.

As she did, a biblical verse came to her unexpectedly. It was a verse that had been a key ingredient of the thesis Veronica wrote for her master's degree. This verse had remained fixed in her mind for months, as she had sought to plumb its depths. Now that same passage was with her again, but this time it wasn't just in her head. Somehow it had found its way into her heart, and was moving through her without the slightest effort:

> "Should you have been banished to the very sky's end, Yahweh your God will gather you again even from there, will come there to reclaim you." (Deuteronomy 30:4)

Veronica knew that God, like the writer of that verse, was calling the beloved. God was pulling David out of pain into joy, out of darkness into light.

For the first time since she had come into the hospital, Veronica took a deep breath, a breath so audible that it startled the clerk sitting at the nurses' station in the hallway outside the room. Veronica's eyes were still on David's tear. But the knife in her soul was gone. Now she was filled with a kind of exultation, like that of the psalmist praising God for the gift of freedom from death:

> For my soul has been freed from death,
>   my eyes from tears, my feet from stumbling.
> I shall walk before the LORD
>   in the land of the living.
>
> (Psalm 116:8–9)

A Gift for an Unnamed Clerk

After a while, Veronica got up to go home. She took one last look at her brother's body. It was hard to leave. Her whole being still ached. David was gone. Gently, she pulled the white sheet over his face. It was sad for her to say good-bye. But in her aching there was also joy: Veronica knew that wherever God was now leading him, David would have no further need of tears.

3

Walking out of the room in which the dead body has been viewed is part of saying good-bye. Should family and friends be allowed to choose for themselves when they are ready to leave, or should that time be determined by doctors, funeral directors, or others who have a schedule to keep?

The wide doors opened automatically for Veronica as she walked out of the hospital. As they closed softly behind her, the clerk at the nurses' station felt something he had not often felt. It was fleeting, but real—a waft of something like peace moving through the heavy-laden atmosphere of the hospital's emergency ward.

> Though the fig tree does not blossom,
>   and no fruit is on the vines;
> though the produce of the olive fails
>   and the fields yield no food;
> though the flock is cut off from the fold
>   and there is no herd in the stalls,
> yet I will rejoice in the LORD.
>
> (Habakkuk 3:17–18)

Crushed Bones Shall Leap for Joy

Several years after David's death, Veronica Shields came to Saint Monica's. She teaches religion and works in the Campus Ministry Office with Father George. David died during Holy Week, the week leading up to Easter. Each year, Ms. Shields finds that her grief over David is most acute during that week.

And now Holy Week has come again, and Ms. Shields is planning the school's Easter prayer service. She has much work to do. Being busy and focusing so much on the mystery of Easter lightens Ms. Shields's sadness about David. Easter gives her hope. She believes that Jesus truly is risen from the dead; she also believes that David rises with him.

Ms. Shields has decided to use a play as the basis for the service. A narrator will read the story aloud as the cast conveys its meaning through mime. Music and art will bring out various aspects of the story as it progresses.

The drama is about a journey. The story begins with the despair of two friends mourning the death of someone they loved. The two friends, downcast and without hope, travel seven miles to their home. On the road, they meet someone who will work a miracle. With their own eyes, they glimpse that which lies beyond the grave.

The cast consists of two actresses and one actor. The two actresses, seniors at Saint Monica's, play the grieving friends. The actor is Sarah's boyfriend, Mike. He has, with hesitation, agreed to play the role of Jesus. With Sarah's ongoing grief over the death of her grandmother, Mike was re-

4
In grieving, times and seasons take on special significance. For Ms. Shields, Holy Week will always be a reminder of David's death. For Sarah, November will always signal her grandmother's funeral. The dead person's birthday, an anniversary, and other special occasions will also trigger feelings and memories in those still living. These occasions can become laden with unremitting pain, or they can become transformed with new hope and new understandings. The nature and degree of transformation will vary with each person. What is your experience with this aspect of grief?

luctant to get into any further drama involving grief. In addition, he was uncomfortable with the idea of being cast in the role of Jesus. To be seen as "religious" by one's peers could lead to being ostracized. However, he agreed to go through with it because he hates to turn down any kind of acting experience, even such a challenging role as that of the Risen Savior.

The Curtain Rises

Finally, the day of the service arrives. The cast is dressed simply, in long white robes cinched at the waist with belts made of colored cord. Mike wears a gold belt. The two actresses wear green belts. The cast is waiting silently backstage. Other than the inevitable foot shuffling and preliminary coughing, the assembly of staff and students is quiet, expectant. The curtain rises.

The auditorium is almost completely dark. Light is shining nowhere but on the stage, with its long road. An art class has painted some lonely looking trees and a few gray stones as a backdrop to the road. The only other thing on the stage is near the front, just off to one side: a small table set with three chairs. On the table is a single white lit candle, three glasses, a bottle of red wine, and a loaf of uncut bread.

The drama begins.

From a distance, a lone flute is heard. Its sound is long, desolate, and mournful. The flute plays for a full two minutes.

Next, a voice is heard. It's the clear, strong voice of the narrator, coming from somewhere at the back of the auditorium.

"On a Friday long ago, an innocent man was nailed to a cross. His name was Jesus. Two criminals were crucified alongside him. Late that same Friday, the dead body of Jesus was laid in a tomb. The tomb was sealed with a heavy rock.

"Two days later, the stone was found rolled away, and Jesus' grave discovered to be empty. What happened to the body of Jesus? We have no eyewitness answer to this question. But we do have a story in which the answer is found."

Two figures dressed in white (the grieving friends) slowly rise, with great difficulty, in a far corner. When they are finally standing, their heads hang low and their shoulders slouch. As they emerge, something becomes visible: painted on the backdrop are three black crosses. The two friends are leaning on each other as they take their first struggling steps on the long road. The sound of the flute fades. The narrator continues.

"They have stopped hoping. Jesus has died."

"Our story begins with two friends, crying and broken-hearted over the death of a man named Jesus. They were shocked and devastated when he was arrested just a few days earlier. They saw him publicly humiliated, tortured, and led up a hill called Calvary. They watched him die. Jesus had been more than just their friend. He was also their Savior—the one who taught them to hope. But now they have stopped hoping. Jesus himself has died. How are they to believe in anything now, or ever again?"

One of the white figures lifts her hand as if to wipe her brow; the other seems to be holding her stomach. The taller of the two friends buckles at the knees, falling on the shorter friend's shoulder. Both sink down slowly into a heap, not far from the three painted crosses.

"Jesus was crucified in Jerusalem. These two grieving friends live in a town called Emmaus, seven miles from the place Jesus died. Today they intend to return home. The journey will be hard. How will they ever rise to move on?"

The two friends are motionless, except that one gently strokes the brow of the other. The sound of chant floats softly over the assembly. The school choir, hidden backstage, is singing without accompaniment. The chant is simple and haunting. Over and over, the choir repeats a single Latin phrase, Veni Sancte Spiritus, *which means "Come, Holy Spirit."*

As the chant comes to an end, the two figures rise painstakingly to their feet. Still supporting each other, they push on toward home.

"The two friends begin to speak to each other about the horrific events of the past few days. They are struggling to make sense of what has happened. How could one they love be ripped from them so suddenly, so brutally? How can their own lives have any meaning for them now? If Jesus was God, how could this have happened?"

A third white figure appears near the crosses. This white-robed figure is wearing a gold belt; he comes upon the two friends.

"'What are you discussing with each other as you walk along?' the stranger asks the downcast pair. They are astounded to think that anyone around these parts could possibly be unaware of Jesus' Crucifixion and death. All the same, they explain it to him. They even tell him how some women found Jesus' tomb empty, and how they came back announcing that Jesus had risen from the dead. But the two friends themselves no longer know what to believe about anything."

Suddenly the gold-belted figure leaps back from the two, his arms waving emphatically. They turn, startled.

"'Oh, how foolish you are, and how slow of heart to believe all that the prophets have declared!' the stranger exclaims. He is amazed at their lack of faith and understanding. He continues to walk with them, opening their minds to help them understand all that has happened to Jesus, all that the Scriptures had foretold of him."

As the three walk along, a moon and stars appear on the wall over their heads.

"As they draw near their village, the stranger makes as if to travel beyond the town of Emmaus. But they reach out to him, asking that he stay with them, as night has fallen."

The three move to the small table, where they sit down. As the gold-belted figure slowly lifts up the lit candle, holding it high above his head, the sound of a soft, low drumbeat is heard. With great care, he lowers the candle to the table. The two friends have fixed their gaze on him. Next, he pours wine into each of the three glasses. Then he picks up the loaf of bread, bows his head over it, breaks it, and gives it to them.

As they reach out, reverently taking the broken bread into their own hands, they look down at it in amazement, then slowly look up into his face again. Just a

few days earlier they saw the body of Jesus, broken and life-less. As their awed gaze becomes fixed on him, the three figures become completely still.

"Then their eyes are opened and they recognize that their companion is Jesus. The man they saw two days earlier—bent over, bleeding, crying out in pain, and, finally, stone-dead—is with them now, risen. Discovering his identity, they think back to what took place as they walked along the road.

"They recall how their hearts seemed to burn with fire inside them as Jesus explained the Scriptures to them.

"They rush back to Jerusalem, proclaiming the Lord's Resurrection."

The Jesus figure picks up the lit candle and leads the other two by its light. The narrator's final speech begins.

"We are a people not with proof, but with hope. Our forebears saw Jesus die, and they went into mourning. But Jesus rose up from death. He appeared to his friends, risen in glory. Astonishingly, they did not recognize him. Not until the breaking of the bread were their eyes opened to the truth.

"When the bread was broken and given, they remembered times their soul and heart had been fed by Jesus. When the bread was broken, they felt their own brokenness. They knew they needed a savior. When they looked up, they saw Jesus.

"Even when we are broken, we can still love, and we can still give. Our eyes can be opened to the truth. We can see God—and ourselves—anew."

The candle is elevated, the three white-clad figures move to center stage, and, for the first time, they speak.

"'Jesus will transform these humble bodies of ours to be like his glorious body'" (Philippians 3:20–21).

"'I am the resurrection and the life: whoever lives and believes in me will not die'" (John 11:25–26).

"'Let me hear the sounds of joy and gladness; the bones that were crushed shall leap for joy'" (Psalm 51:10).

"'Death is swallowed up in victory'" (1 Corinthians 15:54).

As the three white figures quietly turn and disappear, the choir and the whole assembly sing "Amazing Grace." The auditorium lights are turned up as streams of young people come forward and place lit candles from one end of the stage to the other—a sign of Christ's light filling the world.

One Real Hope

Ms. Shields was sitting at the back of the gym as the service was finishing. She identified easily with the two friends' grief and despair at the story's beginning. She used to feel that same kind of heaviness about David. She also understood their inability to recognize Jesus when he first appeared to them along the road. Whenever she indulged her despair, she found it difficult to see God.

However, her heart thrilled at the miracle she saw enacted today. One who had died and been laid in a stone-cold tomb was raised to new life. The Risen Jesus became visible to his friends as they received bread from his hands. Ms. Shields was picturing David, glorified with the glorified Christ. Just then, Mike rushed up to her. He was still robed in white and belted in gold.

Her heart thrilled at the miracle she saw enacted today.

"Ms. Shields, I can't believe how quiet everyone was. When I broke the bread and gave it to the others, nobody was even whispering! No one laughed. I admit, I really didn't want to play Jesus when you first asked me, but something was really happening while we were sitting around that table. . . . Thanks for talking me into doing it."

As the excited actor disappeared into the crowd to find Sarah, Ms. Shields flushed with gladness. It was a grace to see even one student excited about the possibility of Jesus' being real. She sat just a moment longer, quietly meditating on God's resurrection miracle being worked in David, her brother:

> Then I saw a new heaven and a new earth. . . . "He will wipe away all tears from their eyes; there will be no more death, and no more mourning or sadness or pain." (Revelation 21:1,4)

We have no physical proof that Jesus rose from the dead. But we do have stories like the one about the disciples on the road to Emmaus. Each of these stories recounts a similar sequence of events. The Risen Jesus appears to one of his friends. At first, the friend fails to recognize him. Mary of Magdala actually mistook him for a gardener working in the graveyard! Once the friend discovers that this is Jesus, she or he is astounded, then rushes off to tell the good news.

Despite any doubts or unanswered questions we might have, we can say several things for sure. The first is that people reported seeing Jesus die. The second is that these same people reported seeing him again, alive. The third is that we ourselves have one real hope: "that the one who raised the Lord Jesus will raise us also" (2 Corinthians 4:14).

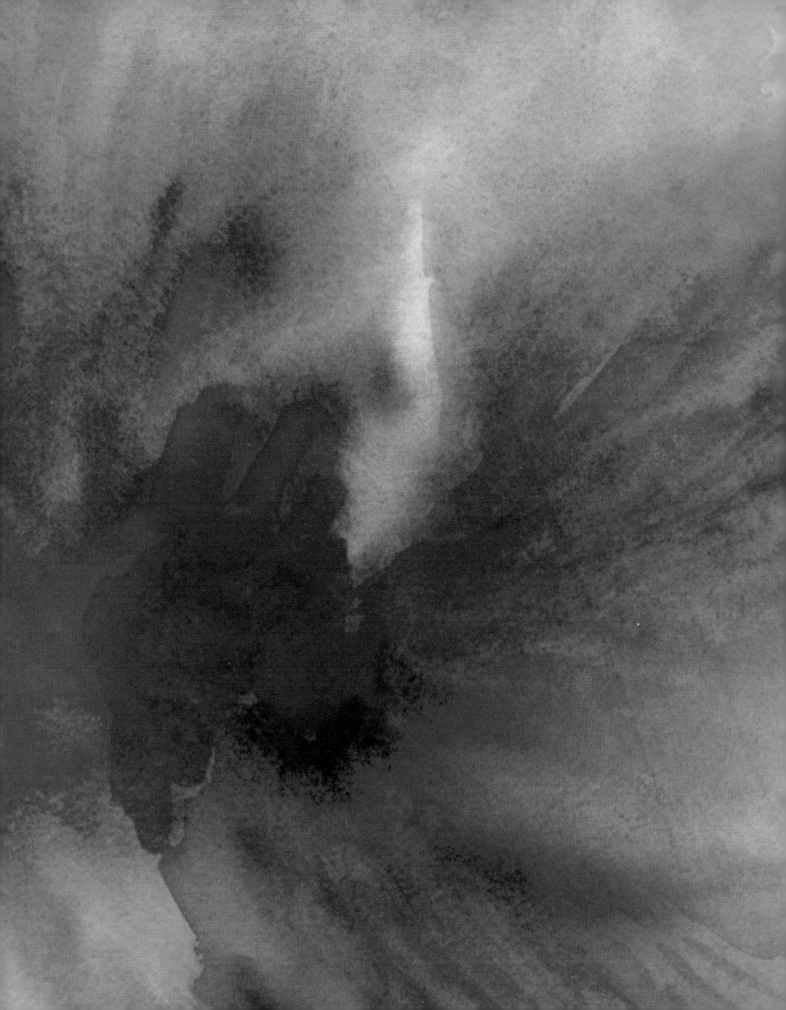

6
What Is Death?

In my happier days I used to remark on the aptitude of the saying, "When in life we are in the midst of death." I have since learnt that it's more apt to say, "When in death we are in the midst of life."
                        —A survivor of the Belsen concentration camp

Death, Desire, Everyday Life

Before reading this chapter, complete the following exercise. Carefully consider each of these situations:

- Nicole loves chocolate. Matthew loves Nicole. He brings her a chocolate bar one morning. Delighted, she bites off as large a piece as is politely possible. Her mouth is immediately filled with crunchy almonds, creamy caramel, and that glorious, rich dark chocolate she adores. Nicole's eyes are closed as she slowly savors the luscious sweetness.

   In your opinion, will Nicole want a second bite? Why or why not?

- Matthew has an extensive collection of CDs and a great sound system. He loves to turn on the music, crank up the volume, and just lie back, drinking in the rhythmic energy. The wildest energy always comes from his newest purchase. Just before settling down to lose himself in his latest rapture, Matthew programs his sound system for continuous repeat. Why?

- Sarah and Mike are in love. Sarah allows Mike to see the deep yearning in her eyes. Then she kisses him. Both feel an instantaneous burst of electricity—intense, tingling, thrilling. Sarah and Mike have never before shared anything so profoundly exciting. They cannot speak. They are blissfully still.

   The next night, Sarah and Mike are together again. Almost immediately, they move into an embrace. As the kissing starts again, the electricity rises.

In your opinion, how long will it be before Sarah and Mike want to do more than just kiss? Why?

You were correct if you answered that Nicole wanted a second bite of chocolate. You were right a second time if you answered that Matthew programmed his system to repeat because just one hearing of his new disc wouldn't be enough. Finally, if you answered that the night was not over before Sarah and Mike wanted to do more than kiss, you were entirely correct.

In each of these three cases, what is most significant is how you responded to the question, Why?

Inexhaustible Human Desire

Perhaps you noticed that in all three of the situations opening this chapter, the young people had a deep desire for more. Just one bite of chocolate could not satisfy Nicole's desire. With each additional bite, her blood sugar level rose, and the pleasurable rush intensified. Nicole wanted more.

Hearing his new CD just once wasn't enough for Matthew. The music sparked a kind of energy in him, and he wanted more of that energy. Soon Matthew will need to buy another new disc—and another, and another, and another—in order to keep feeding his desire for more.

The teasing mix of tender affection and sexual fire Mike and Sarah felt when they were kissing was electrifying, but not enough. In fact, what they experienced quickly whetted their appetite for more.

It's characteristically human to want more. Even babies who have not yet learned to speak have learned how to ask for more. Desire in the human person is so powerful that it cannot be exhausted, not even after one has lived for eighty, ninety, or a hundred years. We will find no food so delicious that it will end our desire for good food. We will find no song so energizing that it will end our need for the exhilaration of music. We will find no sexual pleasure so gratifying that it will end our craving for physical and sexual intimacy. In fact, the more we get, the more we will crave.

No End in Sight

Our desire never ends; our cravings never cease. The human longing for more has no end.

Like Nicole, Matthew, Sarah, and Mike, we search everywhere for satisfaction, for completion, but we never quite find it. As we continue to search, we yearn more and more intensely for whatever will meet our most passionate cravings. Not surprisingly, we suffer more and more poignantly the frustrations and failures of our searching. Incompleteness is hard to bear.

Calvin and Hobbes

by Bill Watterson

Chocolate, music, and sex are almost universally popular. Yet Nicole, Matthew, Sarah, and Mike already know that they want far more out of life than chocolate and music. And they will one day learn that even profound sexual intimacy will leave them longing for something more, something they cannot even name.

Our lives are incomplete. We are insatiable. Where is human hunger meant to lead us? Hunger pulls us more deeply into life. And hunger keeps on pulling. Ultimately it will lead us beyond our self, beyond this life as we know it. Hunger draws us toward that which is beyond our imagination.

How do we reach the unimaginable? There is only one way: we must pass through death. Death breaks all earthly boundaries. Death breaks every known limit. Death fulfills the not-quite and always-passing satisfactions of this life by bringing us into the presence of the source and goal of all our hunger and imagination. Death, therefore, is not just an ending, but a beginning.

Death and God

Does all this mean that we must physically die in order to experience satisfaction?

The answer is an emphatic no. Every human being experiences "tastes" of death throughout life: pain, loss, separation, alienation, frustration, and so on. In other words, each of us "dies" many times while we live. We can respond to these tastes of death in a number of ways. We can allow them to take control of our life, which leads to depression and despair. We can fight against them or deny their existence, actions that will prove to be harmful. Or we can let go of control and allow God to help us through the experiences, with faith in God's love for us and God's desire that these tastes of death will give way to new life. When we respond to tastes of death in this way, we also taste the utter fulfillment of desire that is complete only when our earthly life has ended and we meet God face-to-face.

To better understand the idea of tastes of death, think back to the funeral of Sarah's grandmother. At the end of the funeral, Sarah stood near the grave holding her infant cousin, Corey. Sarah thought about Corey's mom, her aunt Tish, and the day that Corey was born. Labor had been long and difficult—more than fourteen hours. The next day Aunt Tish had told Sarah, "I just wanted to die." But she was smiling as she said it, and Sarah noticed the tender way Aunt Tish caressed Corey as he nursed.

Standing by the grave, cradling Corey, Sarah thought about life and death. She realized that Aunt Tish had tasted

> Death is not just an ending, but a beginning.

death on the day of Corey's birth. To give birth to her son, her heart's desire, Tish entered into the mystery of life, of God, even when it meant going through a physically painful struggle.

For Sarah, the loss of her grandmother was a taste of death. She could fight it, or she could let God help her through it. Sarah was somehow certain that fighting the loss would be destructive. On the other hand, letting go would be hard, but Sarah sensed that through it she would grow.

Each taste of death we experience in life is a call to let go and be open to new life. The death that takes place at the end of life is the final expression of our lifelong tastes of death and our responses to them. This death demands the most radical surrender of all.

In death, the deepest cravings in Nicole, in Matthew, in Sarah, and in Mike will meet their very source. In death, each of these four people will stand face-to-face with God, the maker and fulfillment of all their cravings, the creator and fulfillment of all their hungers, the source and fulfillment of all their desires. (Did it ever occur to you that it is God who created sexuality, as well as the ingredients for both chocolate and music?)

Beyond Our Wildest Dreams

What Jesus Christ has made possible through and beyond death surpasses every human dream, all previous experience, and all possible expectation. But what does this tell us about life today? It tells us that Nicole, Sarah, Mike, and Matthew, and all of us, are best advised to live fully right now, in each moment, with as much courage, openness, honesty, and trust as possible. In this way, we can shape and channel our responses to our natural human hungers so that with God's help, the depths of our human needs can be met.

Hunger is a powerful force. Without proper channeling and shaping, it becomes destructive. Nicole's passion for chocolate could be damaging to her health if she eats too much of it. Matthew, if he becomes too dependent on music, risks locking himself into his own narrow world of unreality and isolation. And for Sarah and Mike's love to grow in a healthy and lasting

manner, it is best that they control their sexual appetites. Engaging in behavior that is not appropriate for them as unmarried teenagers is likely to disrupt or even destroy their relationship.

We must treat our hunger with the utmost care and respect. God wants us to live fully and courageously, with faith and hope. Then we will be able to die courageously, with faith and hope. In death, our life will open up to an eternity of unimaginable happiness and fulfillment.

The beginnings of life-unimaginable are already here, in this world. God has already given us the opportunity to move toward our heart's desire—each time we taste of life and each time we taste of death. The challenge is what we do with what we taste.

God and Human Hungering

Both life and death are mysterious. How can we shape and channel something as insatiable and mysterious as our own hunger? The one who can best answer that is the One who created hunger in the first place. Only God really knows our heart's desire and how it can be met.

Before reading further, pause and try the following exercise: For a few quiet minutes, think about what you most want out of life. What could give you so much happiness that it would be enough for all eternity? When you have an idea of what that might be, silently ask God to help you find it. Now, remaining quiet and still, allow your imagination to soar. Envision how you would feel, right now, if God were to grant your request.

> God wants us to live fully and courageously.

Regardless of how wildly imaginative you were just now, one thing is certain. Whatever you requested of God and imagined receiving was *less* than what God has in mind to give you. "[God] is able to accomplish far more than all we ask or imagine" (Ephesians 3:20).

The path God has chosen for the accomplishment of our dreams is one that inevitably leads us through death. Jesus himself went that route. Through it came resurrection.

Plumbing the Depths

You are now at the halfway point of this chapter and, it is hoped, at least knee-deep in mystery. Are you willing to go deeper? The following questions are tough. See if you can answer them.

- What would you say to a blind person in order to describe the color blue?

- What would you say to a deaf person in order to describe the sound made by a violin? (Assume that this deaf person can read your lips.)
- Imagine that one day you have a son or daughter. Your child has asked, "What is life?" How would you respond? Write your answer in the form of a short letter to your child.

You likely did not answer the above three questions without difficulty. You may not have been able to answer them at all. If it is difficult for us to explain the color blue, how much more difficult must it be for us to explain death?

The Death at the End of Life

As we explore what death is, the mystery gets bigger, not smaller. Everyday tastes of death, and our responses to them, make up a large part of who we are as human beings. If we recognize these tastes of death, they are likely to have a strong influence on the way we understand the death that occurs at the end of life.

Still, only those who have died know for sure what death is and where death leads. Although death and its mystery may terrify, death also fascinates. People of every culture and religion, of every generation and social stratum, have wondered about death. And the wondering continues.

Have you ever thought about what your death will be like?

Does it seem possible that you really will die?

Let's take a look at death from several perspectives.

Near-Death Experience

One day, a seventh-grade boy got a glimpse of his own death. Here is what he said about a waterskiing accident:

> I was skiing with another guy, double skiing. I fell forward and the rope wrapped around my arm. The rope kind of "zipped" and cut all the way through my skin and muscle, all the way to the bone. I was in intense pain and then I passed out. Later I went into shock from loss of blood and the pain of the experience.
>
> Anyway, the driver of the boat didn't know I was still attached so he kept it on full power. For about thirty seconds he dragged me behind the boat and I was pulled underwater.

I remember thinking that I was a goner. Then I remember thinking that I didn't care. The pain went away and although there was a rush of water going by me, I couldn't feel it. . . .

My life flashed in front of my eyes and I specifically remember thinking just how cool my life had been. I thought of my accomplishments so far and all the fun I'd had and was glad to have been here. I knew I was going to die at this point and was willing to accept my life for what it was. Oddly enough it was the most peaceful feeling I have ever had.

Finally the fellow driving the boat figured something was wrong and he shut the throttle down. I came to the surface at that point because I was wearing a life preserver. It was sheer panic at that point. I came back into reality and was in intense pain. They rushed me to the hospital and began treatment. I was in shock for about eight hours and the doctors said I almost died from loss of blood.

What this boy encountered as he approached death is called a near-death experience. Similar stories have been told by people from all walks of life, religious and nonreligious, who have had a brush with death. Although each is unique, near-death experiences usually include one or more of the following elements: a sense of being physically dead, passing through a tunnel, seeing life from a new perspective, encountering warmth and light, feeling safe and loved, feeling free.

People who report such experiences have something else in common. After having come close to death, many feel an increased zest for life and a decreased fear of dying.

Medical and psychological experts do not agree on how to interpret near-death experiences. Some claim they are hallucinatory, brought on by physiological changes in the body. Others believe they are a strong indication that there is a highly desirable afterlife and that God is good and loving. As yet, we have no scientific way of knowing which experts are closest to the truth in their theories about near-death experiences.

Regardless, one point must be kept in mind: A near-death experience is no more than a mere glimpse into death. This phenomenon is likely to leave us with more questions than answers. If so, we are on the right track. We need questions. Without them, we can move no further into the heart of mystery. Our intent is not to invent the truth, but to discover it. The questions that are hardest to answer are the doorways to discovery.

The Starry Night (1889),
by Vincent van Gogh.

Oil on canvas, 29 x 36¼" (73.7 x 92.1 cm). The Museum of Modern Art, New York. Acquired through the Lillie P. Bliss Bequest. Photograph © 1996 The Museum of Modern Art, New York.

Poets, Mystics, and Artists

Perhaps poets, mystics, and artists come closest to expressing the mystery of death. The American poet Emily Dickinson wrote that "Dying is a wild Night and a new Road." Novelist Vladimir Nabokov mused: "Life is a great surprise. I do not see why death should not be an even greater one." French author André Gide wrote, "One does not discover new lands without consenting to lose sight of the shore." Centuries ago, someone cried out, "My being thirsts for God, the living God. / When can I go and see the face of God?" (Psalm 42:3).

Vincent van Gogh, the famous Dutch painter, spoke of a painting he called *The Starry Night*. The piece is rich with contrasts, swirling blues, golds, and blacks. Of his painting, he said:

> To look at the stars always makes me dream as simply as I dream over the black dots of a map representing towns and villages. Why, I ask myself, should the shining dots of the sky not be as accessible as the black dots on the map of France? If we take the train to get to Tarascon or Rouen, we take death to reach a star.

Jesus said to his disciples, "'Very truly, I tell you, unless a grain of wheat falls into the earth and dies, it remains just a single grain; but if it dies, it bears much fruit'" (John 12:24).

In the moments when we drink most deeply of dying and of living, we become poets, mystics, and artists. At those times, we utter something of the mystery of death. After that, we fall silent.

Medically Certified Death

Even though the mystery of death leaves us silent, we live in a world that demands a "workable" definition of death. Medicine, law, and ordinary practicality require that we make daily decisions about when death occurs.

This is necessary for our human functioning. For example, vital organs such as the heart and the liver can be harvested for transplant only after a person's death has been determined and a death certificate issued. But how can we certify something that even the best of our art, poetry, and mysticism can barely capture? What is death, and when is someone dead?

In the end, if a human body began to decompose, we could safely say that the person had died. However, it would be neither possible nor prudent to wait for decomposition before declaring a person's death!

Legally, a medical doctor is the only person who can issue a death certificate. Dr. Sherwin Nuland explains the medical definition of death:

> To be declared legally dead, there must be incontrovertible evidence that the brain has permanently ceased to function. The criteria of brain death currently being used in intensive care and trauma units are very specific. They include such signs as loss of all reflexes, lack of response to vigorous external stimuli, and absence of electrical activity as shown by a flat electroencephalogram for a sufficient number of hours. When these standards have been met . . . all artificial supports can be withdrawn and the heart, if not already stilled, will soon stop, ending all circulation.

Once the brain is said to have died, the body's other organs can be kept functioning through artificial means, but that person's earthly history has come to an end. Without brain function, the human body ceases to be whole. It can no longer serve as a vehicle for human living.

Death is real. As you are reading this sentence, someone somewhere is dying. By the time you finish this paragraph, many more deaths will have taken place. But no matter how carefully we define death for the sake of our medical and ethical systems, our definition will always be incomplete and imperfect. Medicine can ease pain and delay death. However, no medical expertise or any other kind of human enterprise can ultimately prevent death from happening.

Death is real. It cannot be prevented.

"Look, I'm dying. Gotta go."

Drawing by Bruce Eric Kaplan: © 1995 The New Yorker Magazine, Inc.

Some Glimpses of Death

Not a single one of us will avoid this experience we call dying. We cannot know exactly what we will feel or think or sense as we die, but we can learn about others' experiences of dying. What you are about to read are five accounts of actual deaths.

Agony and Peace

The moment of death was, for Mrs. Nouwen, quiet and undramatic. In the final hours of her life, her husband was at her hospital bedside. At the very end, all he noticed was a slight quiver in her neck. He watched as her breathing simply stopped. However, the closing quiet came after several intensely tortured and peaceless days. Her wrenching struggle mystified all who watched her die. Throughout her long life, she had been gentle, loving, generous. Why, they asked, should her dying days be filled with such agony?

Sudden Death

James McCarty was brought to a hospital emergency ward one evening. McCarty was a man with a strong build, an executive in a successful construction company. On this particular night, he was complaining of pressure behind his breastbone. He was pale and sweaty. His pulse was irregular. He had suffered a cardiac infarction, damage to the wall of the heart. Dr. Sherwin Nuland was a young medical student who witnessed Mr. McCarty's death. This is what Dr. Nuland said:

As I sat down at his bedside, he suddenly threw his head back and bellowed out a wordless roar that seemed to rise up out of his throat from somewhere deep within his stricken heart. He hit his balled fists with startling force up against the front of his chest in a single synchronous thump, just as his face and neck, in the flash of an instant, turned swollen and purple. His eyes seemed to have pushed themselves forward in one bulging thrust, as though they were trying to leap out of his head. He took one immensely long, gurgling breath, and died.

Shame and Sedation

A thirty-year-old man came down with a cold that wouldn't go away. Several weeks later, he was told he had AIDS. His health quickly deteriorated, but this was not the source of his greatest suffering. Most acute was his emotional-spiritual trauma. He could not accept that he was to die of

AIDS. So severely distraught was he that his doctors chose to sedate him heavily. In fact, he lived the last few weeks of his life so drugged that he never woke. This young man died without conscious awareness of his own dying. He may well have been entirely unaware of the family and friends who remained faithfully by his hospital bedside as he slipped into death.

Each death is different from every other death.

"I've Accepted It"

Fr. Daniel Berrigan began a ministry to people with AIDS when he was asked by a nun to visit her nephew, who was dying of the disease. The young man, Luke, was a gourmet chef who had once had a restaurant in New York. Throughout his illness, he expressed not anger or shame, but concern for his caregivers—his parents and the nurses who were assigned to spend time with him. After Berrigan's last visit with Luke, Berrigan wrote:

> I was not to see him again. Within days he was in better hands than ours. Faith, though blind with tears, assures us it is so.
>
> His mother wrote: "Luke was the peacemaker in our family. He had great courage and a wonderful sense of humor. . . . Just in the last weeks of his life, when he and I had a quiet moment alone, he took my hand in his and said, 'I know I'm not leaving the hospital, but I've accepted it. It's all right, but I'm concerned for you and Dad. Please don't grieve for me.'"
>
> He meant the request with all his rugged failing heart. And he knew it could not be honored.
>
> "We grieve for him," his mother continued, "but we know that he is with the Lord and at peace and freed from his terrible suffering."

A Loving Farewell

A fourteen-year-old boy with a terminal disease spent his final days in a California hospice. Hospice care is a special way of treating people who are dying. Such care is given either in the person's home or in a special home set up for this purpose. The goal of hospice is to add quality to the days left in a person's life, rather than try to prolong life at any cost. The boy sensed his death was very near. Author Sandol Stoddard wrote about the boy's last day:

> On the day of his death, when his mother came into his room in the morning, the young boy spoke his last words. She asked him what he wanted for breakfast, and his reply was, "A kiss."

These true stories account for just five of the billions of deaths that have occurred throughout history. Among those many deaths are some recurring themes: pain, sorrow, confusion, fear, anger, peace, mystery, love. However, each death is unique. For some, death will come slowly, over a period of years; for others, death will be instantaneous. Some will die alone, some surrounded by friends, some in the presence of strangers. There will be accidental deaths and deaths that are expected, caused by illness. Some will die lucid, others with varying levels of awareness. In death, some will sing God's praises, and others will curse.

The death you are to die will be different from all other deaths throughout human history.

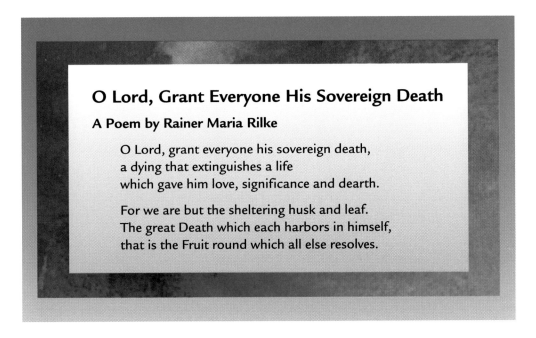

O Lord, Grant Everyone His Sovereign Death

A Poem by Rainer Maria Rilke

O Lord, grant everyone his sovereign death,
a dying that extinguishes a life
which gave him love, significance and dearth.

For we are but the sheltering husk and leaf.
The great Death which each harbors in himself,
that is the Fruit round which all else resolves.

7
Tragedy at Saint Monica's

Grief fills the room up of my absent child,
Lies in his bed, walks up and down with me,
Puts on his pretty looks, repeats his words,
Remembers me of all his gracious parts,
Stuffs out his vacant garments with his form:
Then have I reason to be fond of grief.
                    —*William Shakespeare,* King John

The Night of the Dance

It happened two weeks before Christmas, on the night of the Saint Monica's Christmas Dance, not more than a mile from the school. Six students rode in an ill-fated red car that night.

"Satisfaction"

Keisha and Jerome were in the backseat, their arms around each other. Another couple had squeezed in with them, Scott and Kristen. Nicole and Matthew were in the front seat. They had been a steady couple for months. Matthew thought he was the best thing that had ever happened to Nicole.

Matthew was at the wheel, his beautiful date beside him. He reveled in the knowledge that Nicole was all his. He couldn't take his eyes off her long, sleek black dress and her shining blond hair. Having such a gorgeous girl enhanced his ego. Tonight she was even more of a knockout than usual.

However, even with Nicole's help in bolstering his ego, Matthew's craving for crowd attention and approval was not quite satisfied. So whenever he was in school social circles, he drank. After leaving the dance, the six Saint Monica's students drove to a friend's house for continued partying.

By the time they were leaving the party, it was clear that Matthew had had a lot to drink—in a very short time. Nicole knew he should not be driving. But she was too afraid to say so. After all, Matthew was the center of her life; she was careful never to risk causing a fight. Nicole was so nervous as she slipped into the front seat of the car that she, like Matthew, neglected to fasten her seat belt. It was about one o'clock in the morning.

Intoxication

Saint Monica's Christmas Dance was one of the most celebrated occasions of the whole school year. For that reason only, Matthew's mother had agreed that he could drive her brand-new luxury car that night. Matthew had loved that car from the first moment he had set eyes on it—leather interior, CD player, and state-of-the-art electronic controls. Immediately he had wanted to show it off to his friends. Every time he had watched his mother backing out of the driveway in that great red monster, he had craved command of the wheel.

At last, Matthew was in charge of that magnificent V-8 engine. It was indeed a call for celebration. Absorbing the power of all eight cylinders, he felt fearless and free. The thrill of power combined easily with the dreaminess of intoxication. After the first couple of miles, Matthew felt as if he were riding a runaway roller coaster. He was only vaguely aware that he was actually driving a car.

Matthew did not realize that by getting into the car with him, his closest friends had entrusted their lives into his hands. With the cuddling going on in the backseat, Keisha, Jerome, Kristen, and Scott had quickly forgotten their initial concerns about how much Matthew had drunk. Nicole was mute.

Out of Control

Shortly after they left the friend's house, light rain began to fall. Nicole had been taking drivers' training and had learned to slow down when the first few drops of rain were falling. She knew that at the beginning of a rainfall, the roads immediately become slick and dangerous.

However, Matthew was not the sort of boyfriend whose girlfriend should risk telling him to slow down. She didn't. Matthew sped into the next curve. His exhilaration knew no bounds. He was flying. Practically airborne, he was oblivious to the set of headlights that suddenly appeared as if out of nowhere.

At the top of the big hill near Saint Monica's, the oncoming driver swerved. Nicole screamed. The flame-red car, out of Matthew's control, veered sharply right. It roared over an embankment and slammed head-on into a tree.

Matthew was crushed by the steering column. He died instantly. Nicole was thrown from the car. She suffered massive brain damage. After four days in a coma, she died. Miraculously, Jerome, Keisha, Kristen, and Scott survived. All sustained injuries; Keisha's were the most serious.

Keisha was hospitalized for a full week following the accident. The day she went home, she carried a prescription for high-powered painkillers. Many daily hours of physical therapy lay ahead of her. The doctors said that even with proper therapy, Keisha would never regain full use of her right leg. Her knee ligaments were badly torn, and her ankle was fractured. She was told that with persistent hard work, she could eventually learn to walk without assistance. Basketball was over.

The gorgeous red car was a write-off.

Crisis Response Team

The school and local community were hit hard by news of the tragedy. After all, at Saint Monica's, everyone knew everyone else. Nicole and Matthew had been such an "item"—she so blond and stylish, he so masculine and defiant. The students at Saint Monica's had found it easy to idolize this popular couple.

Nicole's death seemed particularly tragic. For four days following the accident, there had been a glimmer of hope that she would pull through. Then suddenly, like Matthew, she was gone.

The ever-bustling hallways of Saint Monica's became eerily still. The routine activities and life of the school seemed strangely suspended. Even the toughest-looking students and those who always seemed so in charge of their lives were seen crying behind their locker doors. The school's faculty and staff were quickly overwhelmed by their own grief and shock as well as by the urgent needs of so many grieving students.

Saint Monica's, steeped in death denial like many other communities, was ill equipped to deal with the sadness and sorrow of the sudden tragedy. It was a shattered community: shocked, enraged, and confused. Most of its members had no idea how to go about grief-work, no sense of how to deal with the awful calamity that had crashed so suddenly upon their lives.

Any school would have been unwise to try to handle a crisis of this proportion on its own. The staff, therefore, called in an independent crisis response team. The social workers, chaplains, and psychologists on the crisis response team set out to assist as many people as they could. But it wasn't easy. The team could only begin a process that Saint Monica's staff and students would have to continue for a very long time.

How long does grieving take? No one knows. No one can predict its course, nor the afflictions and the gifts to be brought to each mourner. Although sharp pain, upheaval, and sadness gradually dissipate, grieving never really comes to an end. There will always be an incompleteness here on earth. Christians believe that only in God's Kingdom will all things finally be whole.

Shock is a normal part of grief, usually the first part. Shock numbs the sensibilities, acting as a natural anesthetic. Due to shock, people's most intense feelings of loss may not emerge until days or weeks after a death.

1
Reflect on this question: *Does the reality of grief mean that there is no room for hope?*

The Long, Hard Work of Grieving

Several months after the crash, the school's Campus Ministry Office put up posters announcing the start of a Grief Support Group. The group would meet twice a week with Father George and Ms. Shields. Its purpose was to assist students with grief-work.

Denial

It was late April. Kristen, who had been in the backseat with Scott at the time of the accident, immediately noticed one of the posters. Her wavy hair was newly styled. She was pleased to have discarded her glasses for contacts. As she studied the poster, Kristen wondered what grief-work meant. Although she was still suffering from headaches, she had recovered rather well from the accident. She had been relieved that her new hairstyle easily hid the scar on her forehead.

All in all, Kristen was proud of herself—she had been able to go on as if nothing had happened. She felt bolstered by her own stalwart refusal to cry. As for the concerned probing by family and friends, she enjoyed her repeated response: The accident really had not affected her life.

Having read all she wanted to of the poster, Kristen drew her own conclusion: She need not waste any further time on this thing called the Grief Support Group. With her chin up, and feeling quite self-satisfied, Kristen carefully tucked her hair behind her ears and continued on her way.

Kristen was particularly good at living in a fantasy world. Her breakdown would come later.

2
Kristen is in denial. Rather than facing the reality of death and dealing with her own issues, she pretends nothing is wrong. She creates for herself an illusion of self-sufficiency. Denial, as a temporary stage in the grieving process, is normal and healthy; it acts as a regulator of disturbing feelings.

However, ongoing denial is a serious problem, as we have seen in the early chapters of this book. Ongoing denial is like an infected wound: without treatment, the infection worsens, becoming more difficult to treat. Have you ever been in a state of denial?

3
Numbing the emotions is an unhealthy form of escape. The temporary numbness that comes from natural shock is a necessary aid to the initial stages of grieving. But the choice to go on without feeling is a choice against living fully, and it is difficult to reverse this choice later on. If you were to shut down your emotions right now, what might be some consequences in five years? ten years?

Shutting Down

Almost immediately after Matthew and Nicole died, Scott stopped seeing Kristen. Matthew had been the friend that Scott most admired. Scott was shocked that someone as tough as Matthew—or as popular as Nicole—could be struck down so easily. Scott had been equally shocked by the realization that any person could be ripped out of his life—at any time—against his will.

After the funerals, Scott began to spend a lot of time alone. In a flat tone and without facial expression, he told Kristen he didn't love her anymore. He told her he wouldn't be calling again. His was another form of denial. His was a decision to shut down his emotions.

In all, thirteen Grief Support Group signs were posted throughout the school. Scott noticed none of them.

Sensing a Need

Keisha and Jerome were walking past a bulletin board just after eating lunch. They saw one of the signs. The night of the crash, Jerome had been taken to the hospital with a concussion and some minor cuts and bruises, most of which had healed. Keisha continued to have serious difficulty. Physical therapy was grueling, and evidence of significant improvement came very slowly. The pain was constant. Keisha walked but still needed crutches to go any distance. She had to rest often.

Skimming the sign, Jerome and Keisha read that the Grief Support Group was to meet Tuesdays and Thursdays for six weeks, starting in May.

Keisha was the first person to whom Jerome had ever said, "I love you." For Jerome, the accident brought back memories of their frequent breakups. Jerome's running away from the relationship had become a pattern. When Keisha was absent from his life, he felt as if he were dying. Even though they hadn't broken up lately, he was feeling that awful dying feeling again. He had felt it since the night of the crash.

Keisha had talked to Jerome about the accident a few times. She had even cried on his shoulder once. She didn't know much about grief-work, but she thought they should both join the group. Before lunch hour had ended, she had signed up for both of them. Jerome had acquiesced not because he accepted his need for grief-work, but because he wanted to please Keisha.

Sarah's Growing Maturity

Sarah saw a Grief Support Group notice just after English class. Her mind went back to her grandmother's death last fall. Apathetic since the funeral, Sarah had dropped out of extracurricular activities. She did her homework carelessly, or not at all. Her grades were slipping. She wasn't eating properly, and she hardly bothered to comb her hair. Finally, with prodding from her boyfriend, Mike, she had admitted her need for support.

At first, Sarah had been uncomfortable telling her counselor, Ms. Shields, about the personal side of her life. She had gotten along well with Ms. Shields in religion class, but classwork was different—not so personal.

Fortunately Ms. Shields understood the difficulty, even before Sarah explained it. Sarah learned quickly that Ms. Shields was both a good teacher and a helpful listener. She was sensitive, perceptive, and trustworthy. It was easy to see that Ms. Shields, herself, had experienced grief. That helped Sarah feel more understood. With Ms. Shields's assistance, Sarah was able to talk about her grandmother's death. She began to talk about other hurts too, even about feeling abandoned by both her mother and her father.

The gentle warmth with which Sarah's father had looked into her eyes as they had stood beside the hearse had been short-lived. In the weeks after the funeral, Sarah's father increased his hours of work. He had little time for anything but his job. Sarah did not know that by overworking, her father was anesthetizing his own anguish. He was keeping himself too busy to be aware of anything but the next project on his desk, too busy to grieve the loss of his mother, much too busy to notice what was happening with Sarah.

4
Grief-work must be consciously and freely chosen by those who recognize their need for it. Little good comes from forcing people into therapy before they are ready. Do you think Jerome should join the group?

5
Ms. Shields has a compassionate heart, partly because she has grieved the death of her brother in a healthy way. Describe a painful experience in your life that caused you to grow in your ability to understand others' difficulties.

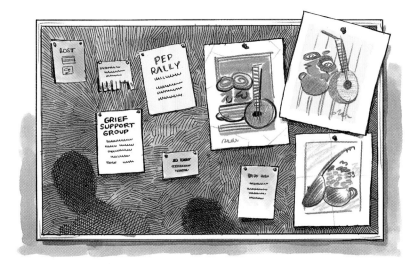

Sarah felt abandoned. Although she still hated to cry in public, she had given in to tears several times during class or in the library. Counseling had launched Sarah on the long journey of delving into her own sadness, anger, and losses. Unlike her father, she had begun to learn that talking about the loss was better than burying it. Sarah knew what grief-work meant—staying conscious through the pain so that it could be transformed.

As she thought about the Grief Support Group, she realized something more. She wanted to hear other people's stories of grief, and she wanted to help those who were facing the same problems she herself had been facing. She decided to register for the group.

A First Glimmer for Simon

Simon had always been an A student, even after his brother's suicide. In fact, after Sash's death, Simon's grades were his highest ever.

Identical twins, Simon and Sash had been born in Egypt. Both had straight black hair and brown skin. As young boys, they had moved with their family to the United States. In junior high, Sash had begun to wear his hair long. At about the same time, Simon had started wearing his hair short. If not for the different hairstyles of the two boys, their teachers could not have distinguished between them.

Sash was fourteen when he overdosed. No one had suspected anything was wrong. Sash had always been quiet, unassuming, and no trouble for anyone. His grades were good, and he always had his homework done. Sash's suicide left his family stunned. They had known nothing of his abuse of medication, his constant need for escape, his inability to deal with his own failures. They had not recognized that in his drive to be perfect and to accomplish everything, Sash felt as if he accomplished nothing. Sash had feared he could never measure up, never be good enough. He felt worthless.

Simon was incapable of dealing with Sash's death. His family's way of dealing with it was to go on as if nothing had happened. They kept their feelings to themselves. Perhaps that's where Sash had learned to suppress his feelings. Simon followed suit. Although he told no one, he made frequent trips to the cemetery. Whether rain, snow, or a bitter wind, Simon stood at his twin's tombstone for long periods of time. He just stood there and stared, motionless.

Simon labored over his homework, meticulously dotting every *i* and crossing every *t*. To onlookers it seemed as if a good student had become a super-student, that the death of his brother had had little or no impact. Simon was like Sash in more ways than appearance—he too could hide his deepest needs and feelings.

Today, as Simon glanced up from the library photocopier, his attention was momentarily captured by the Grief Support Group poster. He quickly returned to his task and loaded another full package of paper into the paper tray. He certainly had no time to be joining any extracurricular groups. The machine kept churning out its copies. Simon didn't look up again.

All these young people could be certain of one thing, whether they knew it or not: We may hide from our own wounds, or we may open them to God's healing touch. Either way, God is filled with tender compassion for us, like a mother who lifts an infant to her cheek. "A bruised reed he will not break . . ." (Matthew 12:20).

6
In Simon's family, denial has become entrenched because the family members reinforce it in one another. Can you think of another example in which a negative quality (for example, low self-esteem, prejudice) is entrenched in a group due to reinforcement? Explain.

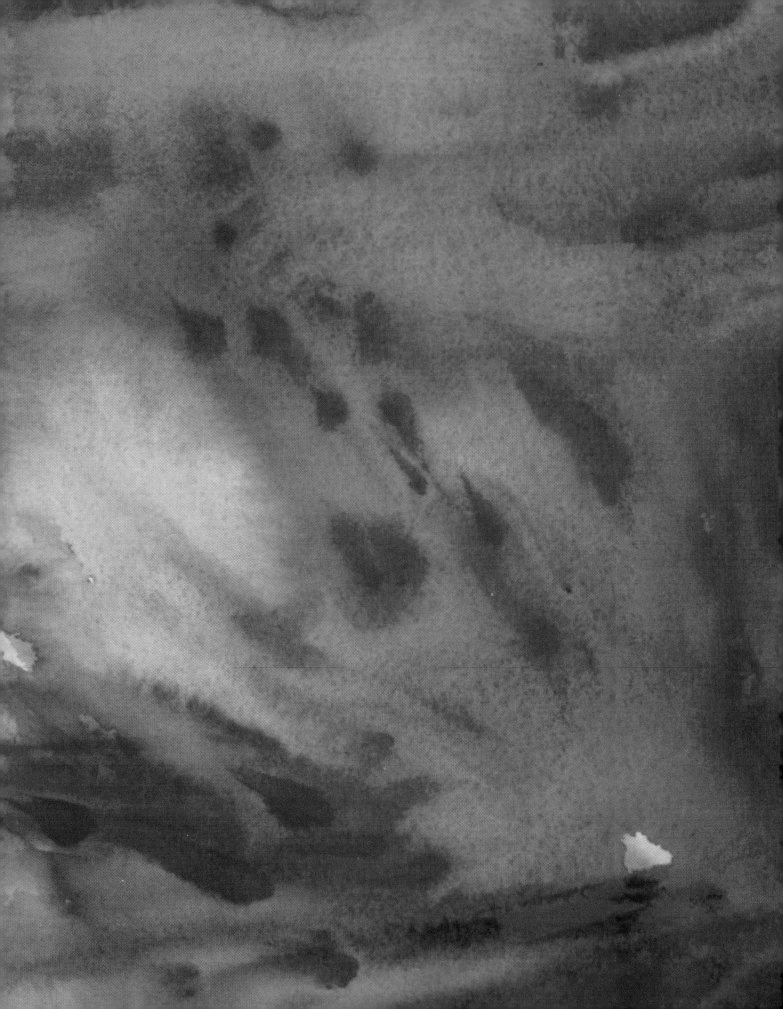

8
Blessed Are Those Who Mourn

All the loves that we love are part of the same love.
All the deaths that we live through are part of
*   the same dying.*
And while we laugh or cry for different reasons,
The sound of happiness is much the same everywhere.
And tears, wept for whatever reason,
Always taste of salt.
                                        —*Marilee Zdenek*

Week 1: Talking About It

Five Brave Individuals

On the first Tuesday of May, shortly before four o'clock, several students gathered outside the Campus Ministry Office. The mood was somber. Keisha was with Jerome; they were leaning together against the lockers. Keisha was leaning because of her injured leg. Jerome was leaning because he wanted to lean with her.

Sarah was there. Although she felt confident, she was also a little nervous. She had become quite at ease in one-to-one counseling with Ms. Shields, but a group would not be the same.

Simon was there too, surprised to find himself on the threshold of an "extracurricular activity." He stood apart from the others. Although Simon kept reminding himself that he had no time for anything outside of course work, he stood stationed at the door of the Campus Ministry Office.

At four o'clock, Father George and Ms. Shields arrived. They had decided to use his office instead of hers—his had more comfortable chairs. Father George often shopped at local thrift stores, and he had acquired an officeful of worn furniture. Students and staff alike could not resist flopping down into one of Father George's big old armchairs. Those chairs felt so good after the hard straight-backs in the classrooms. But no one ever flopped down into the biggest chair, the one by the door. That one was reserved for Father George.

Dawna

As Father George was unlocking his office, one more student joined the group outside the door. It was Dawna, a freshman. Her hair was curly, most of it taupe colored but the ends still bright blond from her peroxide days. Dawna's eyes were an unusual green. And she had "rosebud" lips, lips in no need of the hard red lipstick she always wore. Her complexion was pale, as if she had been ill recently, making her lips seem particularly out of place.

Something sparked in Dawna whenever Father George spoke to God.

Dawna came across as tough, very tough; she didn't bother much with the usual social pleasantries.

A few months back, just after the car accident, Dawna did something she had never done before. She made an appointment to talk to a priest, Father George. She believed she had committed an unpardonable sin, and she felt there was nowhere else to turn. She knew Father George only from his prayers over the school intercom, but something sparked in her whenever he spoke to God.

When she appeared in his doorway asking for counseling, he assumed it had to do with the deaths of Nicole and Matthew. Many students had sought such help. But Dawna's grief had nothing to do with the crash. Father George gave her an appointment for the second week in January. But Dawna didn't show up. She was scared.

When Father George finally located her, he pressed Dawna to reschedule. And she did. Both feared she might cancel again, but she didn't. She kept that appointment and another and another and another.

In April, Father George suggested Dawna join the Grief Support Group. She refused, saying she had no interest in the Saint Monica's crowd. She enjoyed her "outsider" status and preferred to associate with an older, less conventional crowd than could be found at Saint Monica's.

The real reason for Dawna's refusal was fear. She was afraid of what others might think of her if they found out what she had done. Yet Dawna had come to trust Father George. Trust was a new experience for her. Finally, she decided to attend at least the first session.

Sitting in Those Comfortable Chairs

Dawna entered the Campus Ministry Office behind Sarah, Keisha, Jerome, and Simon. All were relieved to get off their feet and into the armchairs.

Seated, Sarah caught sight of a candle on the bookshelf. It was a thick, slow-burning candle set in an old brass holder that had not been polished in a while. Sarah was glad to see a candle in the room. The feeling of comfort from her grandmother's funeral candle had settled somewhere inside her soul. It helped, too, knowing that Mike would be meeting her right after the session ended.

Dawna's favorite chair was the one beside the bookshelf, because that's where Father George kept his sand picture. Every time she came to see him, it had a new pattern in it. Father George must have liked the sand picture a lot. Her heart warmed at the thought.

Father George leaned back and smiled, comfortably taking up his whole chair. A box of donuts on the table caught the eye of the five tense students, as he reassured them,

1

William Shakespeare wrote,

> Give sorrow words: the grief
>   that does not speak
> Whispers the o'er-fraught
>   heart, and bids it break.
> *(Macbeth)*

Do you think speaking openly about our grief is an act of weakness or an act of strength? Why?

"Today we're just going to keep it real light and easy, and we'll finish early."

Ms. Shields had brought the box of donuts. Her passion for chocolate was no secret at Saint Monica's. She enjoyed having that aspect of herself so well known at school. All too often it was assumed that "religious" people like Ms. Shields didn't know how to have fun, didn't allow themselves to enjoy the good things of life. Ms. Shields didn't fit that stereotype.

But Ms. Shields had not brought these chocolate donuts with only herself in mind. She knew from past experience how nervous and uncomfortable students were at the first session of a group such as this. She thought the donuts might help.

Many other students in need of bereavement support had told Father George and Ms. Shields that there was no way they could face a group like this. Cultural denial of death keeps most people away from the subject; they are burdened with the false notion that talking about death *causes* grief.

The five brave individuals in Father George's office were beginning a journey in which they would discover the exact opposite to be true. Grief is the natural human response to loss. Talking about the emotions of grief is a vital part of the healing process.

Tuesday's session passed by with little more than a brief overview of the program, an icebreaker or two, and the polishing off of an entire box of donuts. The overview included a reminder that the group would meet for six consecutive weeks, from four until five in the afternoon on Tuesdays and Thursdays. Two important points were emphasized. The first was about confidentiality. Whatever was said in the group must never go beyond it. Confidentiality was essential to trust. The group members easily understood this requirement and agreed to it.

The second point was about freedom and commitment. The program was not mandatory, but freely chosen. The students were asked to be faithful in their attendance, to complete all twelve sessions. This was for their own sake and that of the group as a whole.

As the students left the session, Simon hoped Ms. Shields would bring donuts again Thursday. He said nothing aloud. But Simon felt that as long as he was in this group, Ms. Shields was a welcome presence. He liked her gentleness and intelligence.

On his way home, Simon made his customary cemetery stop. He stood, expressionless, staring at his brother's grave.

When he got home, he went directly to his computer. As he scrolled down the first page of his homework assignment, he was thinking about his last haircut. Maybe it really had been too short.

Beginning to Talk

On Thursday, Dawna was sick. Both Ms. Shields and Father George were disappointed, but not surprised. They knew that Dawna's attendance record at school had been poor for a while. She was sick a lot. Only Father George knew why. As a result of Dawna's absence, there were only four students at the second session. And there were no donuts.

Today each person was to talk about the death of a loved one—how the death happened and how it felt. Before anyone started, the two group leaders spent some time trying to help the students relax. Father George was glad that Ms. Shields was leading this group with him. Her calming effect was a blessing. The sound of her voice was itself reassuring as she told Sarah, Simon, Keisha, and Jerome: "All we're asking you to do today is to make a start. Tell us whatever you can, even if it's only one sentence, and that'll be enough for now."

Tears of Healing

Father George began by telling them his own story, how his father had died after three years of suffering with Alzheimer's. "My dad was my whole world. Mom died when I was young. When I was a kid, Dad could do anything, fix anything, conquer anything. Putting him in a nursing home nearly killed me. He looked so small in that bed. He couldn't even pull up his own blankets or fluff his own pillow. I'd ask him if he wanted a glass of water, and he'd say he was going out to buy sandpaper so he could do some work in the shed. Wow, that was a killer. He had no idea what I was talking about—and I had no idea what he was talking about. One day he accused me of stealing some money from him. He looked at me as if I were a criminal. That hurt—even more than his actual death."

Ms. Shields spoke next. "My situation was different, but the pain was similar." She told them about how her brother had been taken from her twice: first when he became manic-depressive, and second when he was murdered. "I felt unable to reach David, even while he was still alive. The ache and the powerlessness were so terrible. I've healed a lot, but I still have work to do. I'm glad I'm in this group."

After the two group leaders had finished, Sarah took a turn. She was surprised at her own eagerness to speak. She began, "Grandma's death was almost the worst thing that ever happened to me," and talked for ten minutes about the anger, the shock, and the loneliness. She stopped only to blow her nose and wipe her eyes. When she had finished, she was tired. But she was proud of herself—she had cried in front of people and hadn't minded at all.

She talked about the anger, the shock, and the loneliness.

After Sarah's story, the others shrank back. Secretly they felt afraid to expose themselves as extensively as Sarah had. Unlike Sarah, they had not yet discovered the therapeutic value of expressing painful emotion. They had not experienced the catharsis, or emotional healing, that can occur through giving voice to the soul's depths.

Chains of Control

After some gentle prodding, Keisha managed to say something. "I was in the accident that happened last Christmas. I feel so guilty. I wasn't thinking about anybody but Jerome. I had forgotten about Matthew's drinking. Nicole must have felt so alone. I never saw the other car. All I remember is

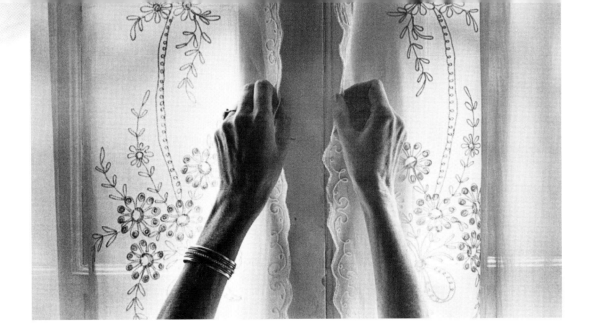

how still everything felt just after the crash. The front of the car was smashed. And Nicole was gone." Keisha broke into tears. Ms. Shields placed a box of tissues within easy reach. Keisha took out a handful and covered her face with them.

Keisha's tears seemed to fill the small room. But there was something in Keisha's tears that had not been present in Sarah's: the sharp sting of guilt. As a result, the group began to feel their own losses far more intensely than before.

Simon was angered by Keisha's breakdown. He felt like hitting her. He wanted to tell her to shut up. But he said nothing. He drove his hands into his jeans pockets and stared straight ahead. Without realizing it, he had assumed his graveyard posture. In his mind's eye, Simon saw himself standing at his brother's grave. Though his facial expression betrayed nothing of his inner torment, Simon's heart was crying out: "Sash, I'm guilty, just like Keisha. You must have felt so alone. I didn't even know. . . . I didn't even know."

Both group leaders sensed in Simon a fierce but controlled reaction. Stiff and statuesque, Simon looked as if he was bound in chains. Father George and Ms. Shields thought it better not to push or prod Simon just then. They made no comment about what they were seeing in him.

In the silence, and feeling somewhat drained by his own inner burst of emotion, Simon had an insight. He knew why he had become increasingly bothered by his short haircut. As children, Simon and Sash had always dressed alike, and their hair had always been cut to the same style and length. But by the time they reached junior high school, Simon wanted a change. He got his hair cut short because he needed to see a difference between himself and Sash. He needed to become more his own person.

2
Grief typically brings with it some measure of personal guilt—Why wasn't I kinder? Why didn't I love more? Healthy guilt leads us to see our failures realistically and to become more loving with others. Unhealthy guilt keeps us bound to past failures, leaving us insecure and less able to love ourselves or others. Can you think of examples in your own life of healthy and unhealthy guilt?

3

A sense of unreality is common in those who are grieving. We can't make sense of what has happened. It even seems impossible. Have you ever experienced a loss that made no sense?

Now he felt guilty about trying to break away from Sash by being different. Sash was dead. No one would ever confuse the two again. There would be no further remarks about how identical they looked. Simon hoped his hair would grow back quickly; he wanted to look like Sash again.

After a long pause, Ms. Shields encouraged Jerome to tell something of his story.

"I was with Keisha and them in the crash. It's sort of un-real I guess. Uh—sorry. I guess I don't feel much like talking today. Matthew was a good buddy. All I got was a concussion." Jerome looked down at the floor and began to study the pattern of lines and squares in the carpet.

Simon wished there were a box of donuts on the coffee table. He wanted it to be Tuesday again, with no demands or expectations. He knew he was going to be asked to speak next. His head was down. He could see only Father George's

huge brown shoes. Father George said, "Simon, it's your turn now."

Simon steeled himself, responding obediently. "I really shouldn't be taking time away from my homework like this. I have a lot to get done before tomorrow. I should never have come." Father George placed his hand on Simon's shoulder. "Simon, just tell us a little bit about what happened."

Simon spoke in a flat voice: "Sash was my twin brother. He killed himself, and I don't know why. That's it."

Neither Ms. Shields nor Father George pushed Simon to go any further. He would, when he was ready. They finished the session with an instruction for the next gathering. Each group member was to bring something that had become precious to him or her, an object that carried feelings and memories about the one who had died.

Because Dawna was absent, Sarah volunteered to give this information to her before the next session.

The Two Sides of Grief

By the time Thursday's session ended, everyone was relieved to file out the door and head home. Ms. Shields had to rush off to a dental appointment. Even Father George was glad to have the first week over with. Alone, he settled back into his chair. He sat and gazed lovingly at the old brass candleholder, which had belonged to his father. Every time he led a support group on grieving, he was brought back to the sadness about his dad. He always experienced a new depth of grieving when he tried to help students come to terms with their own grief. Mourners seem to bring out one another's emotions. Over the years, his father's absence had been more and more integrated into his life. He no longer felt anger toward his dad, but the sadness was still there.

Father George knew that grief has two distinct aspects. It is painful, yes, but it can increase love and expand an individual's horizons. And neither aspect should be denied. Father George had learned to accept his own emotions, their own timing and rhythms, because they are part of the healing action of grieving.

By the time Father George finally pulled himself up to go home, he was wondering about Dawna. He hoped she would be well enough to return by next Tuesday. He cared a lot about his students. He didn't mind that their grief was reacquainting him with his own. He had learned, the hard way, that grief must be faced and lived, not evaded or buried.

4
When we grieve, our emotions can be less controllable, more unpredictable, and easily triggered: by a comment someone makes, by a sad scene in a movie, by something that reminds us of our dead loved one. The greatest healing comes from respecting the rhythms of grief, allowing our emotions to rise up to the surface, and dealing with them as best we can. Of all the members of the Grief Support Group, who do you think finds it easiest to allow emotions to surface? Who has the hardest time letting that happen?

Week 2: Something Precious

Troubled Lives, Special Memories

Dawna returned to the group on Tuesday. As they settled into their chairs, Father George thought about the facts of Dawna's life. She was an only child. Her mother had been eighteen years old when Dawna was born. Following the birth, she married Dawna's father. But the marriage didn't last. From the beginning, Dawna's home life was desolate.

Dawna's father had done his best to stay in touch. When he discovered that his child support money was financing his ex-wife's drinking problem, he sued for custody of Dawna, but he failed. The only way left for him to support Dawna, it seemed, was to provide her with a good education. He paid her tuition so that she could attend Catholic school from age nine. In the meantime, he took a new job and had no choice but to relocate to another city. He called and wrote occasionally, but the emotional distance between Dawna and her father steadily increased. Dawna's mother sometimes assisted the distancing process by stealing letters and neglecting to give Dawna phone messages; she wanted her ex-husband completely out of their lives.

Dawna was asked to tell her story.

The court had ruled that Dawna's mother must receive treatment for her alcoholism, but she remained in treatment for only a short while before starting to drink again. Dawna's father was unaware of the deteriorating conditions of Dawna's young life.

Just before her freshman year began, Dawna became pregnant. Her mother's immediate response was that Dawna should have an abortion. No other possibilities were mentioned. Dawna had an abortion.

It was now the second week of Grief Support meetings. Dawna was asked to tell her story.

Dawna was feeling sick. She had experienced complications following the abortion—occasional bleeding that left her feeling weak. The bleeding finally stopped, but Dawna never felt quite as strong as before. She had skipped both breakfast and lunch today, as she often did, too depressed to care.

Dawna was nervous about revealing her past. As she started talking, she was unaware of having placed her hand on her abdomen.

"Last fall, I had an abortion." Feeling an unexpected surge of remorse rising up as if to choke her, she quickly added: "Lots of people do. It's perfectly legal." Dawna preferred to justify herself than to go on feeling that awful remorse. "Father George, I don't want to say more than that. I don't have to, do I?"

Revealing What Is Precious

Dawna and the others were reassured that they need say only as much as they wanted. Dawna relaxed a little.

On the table was a curious collection of things, each bearing memories of someone now dead—a gold ring, a baby's pacifier, a photograph of Nicole and Matthew, a worn black leather book, a pill bottle, and a sealed envelope.

After Dawna's abrupt disclosure, Ms. Shields asked the group members to reflect quietly on what they had chosen to bring and why. A few tears flowed in the silence, though Dawna, Jerome, and Simon remained straight-faced. Simon was alarmed to think that crying might be a regular part of this group.

After a while, Sarah reached out and picked up the gold ring. "I just have to put this back on my finger." Feeling better, Sarah explained about the ring. "Grandma adored roses. Even though she spent a lot of time on her computer, she still had time for her rose garden. She used to love seeing the

5
Grief results from loss. When we've lost something or someone, we may fear further losses. In our anxiety, we may become overly controlling—of others, of ourselves, of our possessions. We need instead to trust, to cherish, and to hold dear, even though loss will surely happen again. How have you responded to loss in your life—with anxiety or with trust?

backyard in June. That's when it started to come to life with the first few rosebuds. Double Delight. Tropicana. Queen Mary. Blue Moon. I can't remember all their names, but Grandma knew every one. Her wedding ring had roses engraved all around it, but they're kind of worn down now." She looked at her hand. "I lost this ring, once."

Mention of the lost ring brought back deeper feelings of loss. Sarah started to cry again. "When Grandma died, I felt like I died too."

Father George helped Sarah explore the meaning of the ring. With the group's help, she began to see that wanting to keep it on her finger was like wanting to hold on to all things dear, lest something else should be taken from her. The group easily identified with that sentiment.

A few minutes later, Keisha picked up the photograph of Nicole and Matthew. In the picture, they were kissing under a big bunch of red and green balloons in the dance hall. Keisha talked about how she and Jerome had become a foursome with Nicole and Matthew. She tried to describe some of the fun times they had enjoyed together, but it hurt too much. She couldn't go on. She returned the picture to the coffee table.

Being Gentle with Ourselves

It was ten to five. Father George and Ms. Shields had agreed never to run overtime. Their concern was not only that their students meet the bus on time. They knew that grief-work was intense and heavy going. It had to be taken in small steps. The flow of memories and feelings brought out by the sharing of what was precious had to be treated with the utmost care. Therefore, with only ten minutes remaining, it was too late to ask another person to start speaking.

No one did any talking during the last ten minutes of Tuesday's session. Instead, Father George strummed softly on his guitar. He could play only a few tunes, but he loved to strum. He played his guitar as though he were stroking a beloved pet. The others watched and listened as Tuesday's session came to a quiet close. All took their precious belongings with them that night.

Running Away

On Thursday, all but one of the sacred belongings reappeared on the coffee table. The baby's pacifier was missing. So was Dawna.

Eruption

Thursday's session began with a recording of soft, wandering piano music. Then Sarah spoke. With no awareness of what she might evoke in Simon, she said to him: "Talking about my grandmother's ring helped me. Maybe if you told us about your envelope it would help you too."

Simon was unaccustomed to having girls speak to him, so he felt obligated to answer immediately. Looking down, he mumbled hurriedly, "What's in the envelope belongs to my brother."

Sensing Simon's need to escape to the background, Father George turned to Jerome: "Could you tell us what this photograph means to you?"

"Matthew was a great guy," said Jerome. "He never did anything wrong. I liked everything about him. And Nicole too."

Ms. Shields thought that Jerome's words sounded noble, but it seemed to her that something other than mere nobility was at work under the surface. She thought for a moment, trying to formulate a question that might help Jerome explore his underlying feelings.

Keisha didn't tell the group what she had been thinking as Jerome talked. She couldn't help remembering how many times Jerome had complained to her about Matthew's showing off and dominating their crowd. Jerome had also said many unkind things about Nicole. It bothered him that she swallowed everything without ever challenging Matthew on his bad behavior. Keisha was well aware that Jerome did not believe Matthew and Nicole had been perfect. She was puzzled.

Ms. Shields finally came up with her question—a tough question, but she asked it gently: "Jerome, I'm surprised to hear you say that Matthew never did anything wrong. Are you being completely honest with yourself? According to the police report, Matthew was responsible for the accident."

Jerome felt as if he had been stung. The thin veneer covering his guilt had suddenly been stripped away. He stood up and shouted: "Of course he was responsible. But he was drunk! And I knew it! Okay? I admit it. That's what you want me to do. I admit it: I'm guilty. I wasn't drunk when he took the wheel! I wasn't drunk! I had a responsibility too!"

Jerome stormed out of the room.

Jerome stormed out of the room and slammed the door behind him.

Keisha was alarmed by Jerome's abrupt exit. "I can't believe he did that," she said, blinking back tears.

In time, Keisha would understand that those who are grief-stricken often deny reality, especially if they feel as guilty as Jerome was feeling. Underneath Jerome's praise of his two dead friends was his shame. Although he had not admitted to it before today, he knew he should not have allowed Matthew to drive drunk. But it was much less painful for Jerome to paint a rosy picture of Matthew and Nicole than to face his own culpability.

For a moment, Ms. Shields wondered whether her questioning of Jerome had been appropriate. In truth, almost anything could have triggered Jerome's exit. After all, he had come not to grieve but to hold on to Keisha.

The discussion following Jerome's eruption was rich with insight. The two group leaders helped Keisha to name her own mixed feelings about what Jerome had just done: feelings of anger at his constant need to run away, feelings of caring and concern for what Jerome must be going through, feelings of shame about her own guilt. After all, she too had been sober enough to recognize Matthew's impairment. Like Jerome, she had done nothing.

Wake Up, Sleeper

After discussing the desire we all have to run away, and how to deal with it, Father George opened the small black leather book, the precious belonging that he had placed on the table. He read aloud, "Wake up, sleeper, rise from the dead, and Christ will shine on you." Then he said: "I used to read that line to myself every time I left the nursing home. I knew there was no cure for my dad's illness, but I wished so much that he could 'wake up' and recognize me just one more time. I had so much I wanted to tell him. I kept asking God to let his mind function again, just once more before his death."

"I felt like that with David," Ms. Shields said. She picked up the pill bottle from the table. "This was David's prescription. It's a bottle of pills. Almost full. David hardly ever took them. This medication helps sufferers of manic-depressive illnesses. But David wouldn't take it. Whenever I tried to persuade him, he would tell me he wanted to make it on his own, without help."

She shook the pill bottle lightly. "I hated to think that David need not have suffered as much as he did. But it's taught me something about myself. I need people to help me when I'm down, when I'm mixed up, when I've made mistakes. And I need God. It's okay to need."

Jerome's sudden exit had startled Simon. Simon himself had been tempted, more than once, to run out of the room. Simon was proud of himself for having had the guts to stay. Still, he wished he could suit himself in a kind of armor. Now he was the only guy in this group of girls, and he would have to work even harder at keeping his feelings hidden. Looking at his envelope on the table, he thought about reinforcing the seal with some tape. He wanted to shield himself from the group's probing eyes. But what Simon did not yet know was that he really wanted to shield himself from his own eyes.

Five o'clock came, and the second week ended.

6
Grieving makes us more aware of our limits, our needs, our dependence on God. Allowing ourselves to be supported and cared for is a big part of the healing process. Is it easier for you to acknowledge your needs or to resist them?

Week 3:
Letters from the Heart

Stay Awake with Me

Jerome did not return. Ms. Shields knew that his absence was significant for the group. In talking about what had happened with Jerome, the group members made a discovery about themselves: They often wished they could quit the grieving process. But they also understood that they needed their grieving. Though the first few sessions had been difficult, the students were learning that it is better to face our emotions and to risk with others than to become isolated and cut off.

Jerome had declined the risk.

Dawna was back, and so was the baby's pacifier. Father George was pleased. Simon and Dawna had yet to speak about their precious belongings. Simon had reinforced his sealed envelope. He was sure there was no risk of its coming open.

Simon elected not to talk any further about his envelope. He was secretly relieved to find that no one was trying to force him. Simon's precious possession remained on the table with the rest. Although he was encouraged to talk about it, he was reassured that the choice was his. Simon liked that.

Sarah couldn't help noticing that Simon had started to brush his hair forward rather than back; his hair looked longer, more like Sash's had been.

Dawna's Story

Today Dawna wanted to talk. Her aloof condescension was wearing off. She told them how she had gotten to know one of the older guys at the donut shop where she worked the summer before freshman year. She used to hang around there after work. Anything was better than going home. She had enjoyed his attentions; that was a new experience for her.

"But one night he talked me into going to his place after work. His parents were away. We started fooling around, and then we had sex. From then on, that was all he wanted to do with me. I had to quit my job to get away from him." Dawna told them how her mother had caught her doing a home pregnancy test in the bathroom, and how the decision about abortion had been made quickly.

Dawna felt no shame about having gotten pregnant. But the gradual realization that she had aborted her own baby bothered her a lot. She didn't tell them about the abdominal pains she had suffered. But the pain had scared her, made her realize the seriousness of what she had done.

Then she picked up the object she had brought, a pacifier. "At first I didn't know what to bring. My baby never lived long enough to need any clothes or toys or blankets." Saying that out loud made Dawna feel like dying inside. Leaning forward, she moaned: "I didn't have any souvenirs, so I bought this last week. No baby ever used it." Dawna's pale face went nearly white. She closed her hand so tightly over the pacifier that her whole body shook.

It was a long time before Dawna relaxed her hand. Exhausted, she fell back into her chair.

"Dawna, out of all the things you could have bought, why did you choose a pacifier?"

Keisha's question startled Dawna, but Dawna's response was quick: "Because it's supposed to make crying stop!" She threw the pacifier hard against the wall. It landed in the corner. No one moved. "I wish something could take this pain

7
Grief comes out when it's ready. No one should ever be forced to say or do too much too soon. What might be some negative consequences of forcing grief?

8

For a person in mourning, the pain can seem endless. But it isn't. And as the pain slowly changes, new possibilities come to light. Choose a member of the Grief Support Group and speculate on the new possibilities that may arise, through grief, in her or his life.

away, but nothing does! Nothing!" The others in the room were wide-eyed; hearts were racing.

Dawna's outburst opened the floodgates. In the following discussion, it became clear that Dawna was feeling maternal toward her lost child. Dawna ached to protect and to nurture. Her own need to feel protected and nurtured also came out. In her trauma over the abortion, Dawna wished so much that someone could hold her like a baby.

At four-thirty, Father George's long arm reached all the way across his desk to a pile of paper. The paper was an uncommon mauve color. Each person was given a sheet. At the bottom of the sheet, there was a single line of small print: "'My heart is ready to break with grief. Stop here, and stay awake with me'" (Matthew 26:38).

Father George told the group about the passage from Matthew's Gospel: "This is what Jesus was feeling the night before he was executed. He was aching all over. He knew there was no way to stop the pain. All he wanted was for his friends to stay close by. That much, at least, we can do here, for each other." He knew that Dawna's outburst had touched raw feelings in every member of the group.

A Heart, Broken with Grief

Father George strummed on his guitar and asked the group to think about writing a letter on the mauve sheet of paper.

He gave careful instructions: "One of the hardest things about death is that we can't have any more conversations with the one who has died. We can't just sit down and have a good talk the way we used to. And this is even harder for Dawna because she has never had even a first conversation with her child. All of us probably have lots of things we want to say to our loved one. This letter is a chance to say what you want to say. Your letter could be as short as two or three lines—or even one. Or as long as you want. It's up to you."

"My heart is *already* broken with grief," Dawna thought to herself.

Ms. Shields, of course, had no way of knowing who was thinking about what. Still, she was sure all could identify with Jesus' need for his friends to stay with him in his suffering. The worst suffering is that which is endured alone. Ms. Shields saw that these students were beginning to understand why this group was called a "support" group; they had begun to experience for themselves the same kind of support and comfort Jesus had begged of his friends.

As Ms. Shields turned toward her own sheet, she recalled David. It saddened her, even now, to realize that he had been so alone in his illness, so alone in his death.

After a few minutes, Father George took a mauve sheet for himself. He wrote: "Dear Dad. Wish so much I could talk to you again. Wish I could imagine what it must be like for you to wake up in heaven. Wish you could tell me what it's like to be so close to God."

Everyone else started to write too. For a few minutes, the only sound heard was that of pencils scratching. Soon, however, that sound was accompanied by the familiar idling of the late bus. It was nearly five o'clock when Dawna stood up. She went over to where the pacifier lay. Her shoulders were hunched as she looked down at it. She bent to pick it up. Tenderly dusting it off, she returned to her seat. Somehow everyone felt a little better.

The students were instructed to take home their mauve paper, but to bring it back on Thursday.

Give Us Courage

On Thursday, all the precious belongings were present, but not all the letters. Simon's letter was not there. Neither was Sarah's. Simon said he had forgotten his. Sarah said she had an important reason for not being able to bring hers.

Father George extended his hands over the coffee table. For a second, he looked into the pain in Dawna's eyes, then he closed his own. "God of mercy," he said, "look with compassion on our precious symbols and letters. Console us in our hurting. Give us courage enough to look inside ourselves. Give us faith enough to believe that you are here, helping us, bearing in yourself the pains we ourselves now bear."

His prayer had come straight from the heart. It brought solace to the group.

Love and Be Loved

Sarah began to explain about her letter. She had given it to her father. She explained that although her father was not physically dead, he seemed dead to her. In some ways, Sarah had more to say to her father than to her dead grandmother.

Sarah explained: "Uncle Phil phoned my dad a few times after the funeral, but Dad never returned any of the calls. Lots of people were around at first, but afterward everybody seemed to disappear. You know, Daddy has even

Typically, mourners are surrounded by family and friends at the beginning. Very soon, though, this support may disappear. It's not easy to journey with the bereaved; many turn away when they are needed most. What reasons might be behind this tendency to turn away?

lost me, in a way. Since he's always at the office, he hardly ever sees me anymore. He's so alone. But that really makes me mad because it doesn't have to be that way. I'm not dead, and neither is he. I wrote him a really long letter—the sheet you gave us was only the first page."

Sarah knew she couldn't take away her father's pain any more than anyone else could take away hers. But she wanted her father to know that she loved him—and that his distancing angered and hurt her. "I told him all the things I really wanted him to hear. I cried a lot, and it felt good."

Sarah's disclosure touched something in Dawna. She turned to Sarah and ventured a question: "What did your dad say about the letter?"

"I don't know. I haven't seen him in two days. But I'm not giving up on him. I know he'll read it." Sarah kept talking about her father. She was still hurt and angry. The more she talked, though, the more she felt a kind of warmth inside her, the same warmth she had felt the day of her grandmother's funeral. She told the group about the warmth she had felt as her father had looked so gently into her eyes that day. For now, at least, the memory was enough to keep her going.

Dawna, excited by what was happening with Sarah, offered an insight. "Wow! You felt that warm feeling again, and your dad wasn't even being nice to you. Writing him that letter gave you the same feeling you got from him at the funeral. That's amazing. I bet it wasn't just your dad's love that you were feeling that day—I bet it was your love of your dad, too—and that's what's helping you right now."

Dawna had helped Sarah make an important discovery. We need to love as much as we need to be loved. Sarah was glad that Dawna was in the group. And Dawna felt more and more that she belonged here. It was a good feeling.

Owning the Feelings Brings Healing

Dawna's letter was the only other one talked about on Thursday. Hers was written to her unborn child. In the letter, she named her child Mary. Dawna had not known her baby's sex, but she felt in her soul that it was a girl.

Dawna said she had rewritten her letter several times, and was anxious to read it out loud to the group. Somehow it seemed to her that reading it aloud gave her baby a better chance of hearing it: "Dear Mary. This is the first time I've ever called you by your name. I hope you like it. I picked it because it's an old-fashioned name—not like the made-up ones you hear on TV. Mary is a real name. I know that you're real. I wish I could have seen what color your eyes

Dear Mary,
This is the first time I've ever called you by your name. I hope you like it. I picked it because it's an old-fashioned name - not like the made-up ones you hear on TV. Mary is a real name. I know that you're real. I wish I could have seen what color your eyes would be - maybe green like mine. I bet you got curly hair like me. I'm sure you will never be able to forgive me, but I wish so much that you could. I wish I could have fed you and changed your diapers. I would have tried really hard to be a good Mom for you.

From Dawna

would be—maybe green like mine. I bet you got curly hair like me. I'm sure you will never be able to forgive me, but I wish so much that you could. I wish I could have fed you and changed your diapers. I would have tried really hard to be a good Mom for you. From Dawna."

Dawna had attempted to sign the letter "Mommy," but couldn't.

For the rest of Thursday's session, the group talked about Mary. Dawna came close to tears a few times, but managed to control herself. Even so, Father George had never before seen so much color in Dawna's face. It was a good sign. Dawna had taken two big steps—she acknowledged both her need for Mary's forgiveness and her desire to have been a good mother. Talking about Mary helped Dawna realize that the baby was real, as was her grief over the loss and her remorse over the decision to abort. It also brought Dawna into the hearts of all present.

At the end of Thursday's session, everyone was tired, as usual. However, they went home not so much aware of their fatigue as touched by Dawna's love of Mary. Dawna's love seemed to outweigh her shame. That brought hope.

Stirring the Depths

At the end of week 3, the grief support program was half over. Father George and Ms. Shields sat down to compare notes on how it was going.

Though filled with pain, Dawna seemed to be blossoming. And her progress was stirring the depths of the others.

Jerome's disappearance had been distressing. He hadn't even come back to tell them he wasn't returning. Ms. Shields stopped him after class the day following his sudden exit from the group. Jerome offered no explanation, but he made it clear he considered the group a waste of his time.

As for the rest of the students in the group, they seemed to be moving forward. Slowly but surely, each at a different rate, these young people were walking the healing path of grief. Perhaps Jerome's decision to leave when he did was a necessary part of his journey. Working through grief cannot be forced, only led and encouraged.

Both Father George and Ms. Shields would look for informal opportunities to stay in touch with Jerome. They hoped that in the hallway or the cafeteria they would be able to maintain some form of contact. As things went, however, even that was not going to be possible.

Father George and Ms. Shields talked about Simon's need to have his hair look like Sash's again. They knew it

10
For Dawna, hope has emerged through loss. Have you ever experienced hope in a situation in which hope seemed impossible?

11
It is common for people to "drop out" of the grieving process. Grief-work is arduous and requires a real commitment. Compare grief-work with another difficult challenge that requires a commitment.

was not unusual for someone to try to take on characteristics of a loved one who had died. For Simon, this was probably a way of holding on to Sash. What was equally clear was Simon's need to hold on to his well-taped envelope. In fact, Simon would let go of almost nothing; he kept everything locked up and tightly reined in.

The two counselors hoped that Simon would let go a little in the next three weeks. It takes a lot of energy to repress intense emotion. No wonder Simon looked tired all the time.

12
Human beings are a unity of body, mind, and soul. All dimensions of ourselves need to take part in grieving. When we block ourselves from our own depths, we may develop physical ailments—headaches, abdominal pains, fatigue, sleeplessness. Allowing ourselves to grieve is a necessary part of physical, spiritual, and emotional health. At this point in the process, what advice would you give to Simon?

9
They Shall Be Comforted

The world breaks everyone, and afterward many are strong at the broken places.
    —*Ernest Hemingway*, A Farewell to Arms

Week 4: In Memoriam

Rage and Prayer

Funerals are not popular occasions; we attend them only when we must. Funerals hurt. Yet, at its very heart, a Christian funeral celebrates the most cherished hope of all: that death is not the end. Funeral memories are an important part of grief-work. For this reason, Ms. Shields and Father George decided that the fourth week of the Grief Support Group would focus on the funeral experience.

One group member was without such an experience. There had been no funeral for Dawna's baby, aborted at fourteen weeks. When Dawna's pregnancy was discovered, neither Dawna nor her mother spoke of an "unborn child." They spoke, rather, of an "it," of something that had to be "gotten rid of." After the abortion, no one referred to Dawna's baby as a "child who had died." No funeral or memorial service was held.

Colored Ribbons and Gold Edges

It was Tuesday afternoon. Ms. Shields was holding a heavy, dark blue book. Keisha noticed the title engraved on the cover: *Funeral Rites*.

It seemed appropriate to Keisha that a book of death rites should be heavy, dark, and blue. Keisha had been finding her own grief heavy and dark. She had found it particularly difficult to accept Jerome's dropping out of the group. Not only had this reinforced his weakness in her eyes, but it made her feel more alone with her grief. She felt a great gulf between herself and Jerome.

Keisha noticed, coming from inside the book, colored ribbons—orange, yellow, and red. And the pages were all edged with gold. The book itself was a contrast of darkness and brightness. Keisha was experiencing a similar contrast within herself. Old feelings of loss and abandonment were mixed with new feelings of personal strength and hope.

Keisha was in the process of making a discovery about grief. Death and life go together. We rise up through grief by moving through the very heart of our suffering, not by trying to bypass it. The heart of Keisha's suffering lay in her guilt and anger.

She needed to move through those difficult feelings in order to forgive herself for having ignored Matthew and Nicole the night of the crash. She also needed to forgive Jerome for his weakness, for his inability to be all she needed him to be. She had to accept Jerome's decision to drop out of the support group. She had to allow him to follow his own path through grief.

Moving out of guilt, Keisha would regain some of the self-esteem she had lost. Eventually she might even consider the possibility that God had not abandoned her—not when her dream of going to medical school had seemed to be in ruins, not when she and Jerome had broken up, not even when she had failed Matthew and Nicole the night of the accident.

But something else was bothering Keisha. She said to the group: "Last night someone told me that grief takes five years, and you have to go through seven stages of it altogether. If you miss any of the stages, you never get over it."

A state of alarm overtook Keisha's peers as a new fear surfaced in them; they might fail in what they were supposed to do. Neither Father George nor Ms. Shields was alarmed, though. They saw Keisha's concern as an opportunity for the group to discover something both freeing and encouraging.

"One of the marvelous things about human beings," Father George began with a smile, "is that we're all so similar in how we react to things—and yet so very, very different." Ms. Shields and Father George told the group some interesting things about research in the area of grief-work. Various professionals have studied grief and written about it. No two ever come up with exactly the same understanding, and no two use exactly the same terminology. These professionals explain the grieving process in different ways. Some speak of stages, others of phases, and still others of tasks or successive reactions of grieving. The two group leaders pointed out that some schema suggest five steps, some twelve, some nine, others seven, and so on. In short, the group learned that no single formula can fully explain all individual experiences of human grieving. The wonderful thing is that we can learn valuable information from all such views and schema, as long as we keep our own unique and personal experience in mind at the same time.

The grieving process can be explained in different ways.

Before the Grief Support Group had even started, Ms. Shields and Father George knew they would *not* be using any one particular theory of grief-work with this group. Rather, they would use their knowledge of the wide variety of grief-work theories and of Catholic teaching to help them understand each person's needs and rhythms as she or he moved through the process of grieving. And above all, they would listen prayerfully for the promptings of the Spirit, allowing God to help them guide each young person as she or he needed.

Everyone felt relieved. They felt less burdened by expectations. And they were comforted by the idea that individuals can move through the various challenges of grief in their own way and in their own time.

Ms. Shields read aloud from the gold-edged book: "Merciful Lord, you know the anguish of the sorrowful, you are attentive to the prayers of the humble. Hear your people who cry out to you in their need, and strengthen their hope in your lasting goodness."

Describing the Stages of Grief

Grieving is not scientific. It is not predictable or quantifiable. Various experiences of grieving can be described, and the similarities noted, but each person responds to loss in her or his own unique way.

Even so, many professionals in psychology, medicine, counseling, and ministry have tried to develop general descriptions of the stages, or phases, of grieving. Such descriptions can help us understand our own experience of grief, or that of a friend or relative. However, they are not to be understood as perfect or complete pictures of grieving—not all stages will be experienced to the same degree in all people, or in the same chronological order. In addition, it is normal for stages that have been experienced to sometimes reappear at a later time. Here are summaries of three approaches to understanding grieving.

A Ten-Stage Approach

1. *We are in a state of shock.* Initially, our shock serves as a temporary escape from reality.
2. *We express emotion.* We should allow ourselves to express the emotions we actually feel.
3. *We feel depressed and lonely.* This is a normal part of healthy grief, and it will pass.
4. *We may experience physical symptoms of distress.* Illness can be caused by an unresolved grief situation.
5. *We may become panicky.* If we are unable to take our mind off our loss, we may panic and think we are abnormal.
6. *We feel a sense of guilt about the loss.* We should face our guilt, because if it remains unresolved, it can make us miserable for years.
7. *We are filled with anger and resentment.* We must admit our anger, work through it, and not allow it to take us over.
8. *We resist returning.* If the state of grieving becomes too familiar, we may resist returning to our everyday life.
9. *Gradually hope comes through.* Other experiences in life begin to be meaningful again.
10. *We struggle to affirm reality.* Although life will never be the same following loss, there is much in life that can be affirmed.

(Summarized from Granger E. Westberg, *Good Grief*)

"I Hate That!"

Suddenly, Simon spoke. "I hate that!" The group was stunned. Simon rarely spoke of his own accord. They were surprised by the forcefulness of his tone as he continued: "Why would they use a dumb word like *goodness* for God? God has nothing to do with goodness. I hate those stupid prayers."

Simon swept up his taped envelope, which had been stationed on the edge of the table directly in front of him. He unzipped his backpack and jammed the envelope down the side, burying it under his textbooks. Then he zipped the bag shut.

Father George turned to Simon. "You sure wanted that out of sight in a hurry."

A Five-Phase Approach

1. *Shock.* Characterized by disbelief, confusion, restlessness, feelings of unreality, regression, helplessness, and a state of alarm
2. *Awareness of loss.* Characterized by separation anxiety, emotional conflicts, an acting out of emotional expectations (for example, setting a place at the table for a deceased spouse), prolonged stress
3. *Conservation, withdrawal.* Characterized by despair, withdrawal from others, diminished social support, helplessness
4. *Healing—the turning point.* Characterized by assuming control, restructuring one's identity, relinquishing roles (for example, relinquishing the role of son or daughter when a parent dies), forgiving, searching for meaning, finding hope
5. *Renewal.* Characterized by having a new self-awareness, accepting responsibility (for example, taking care of tasks, such as maintaining social connections, that were previously handled by the person who has died), learning to live without the person we have lost

(Summarized from Catherine M. Sanders, *Grief: The Mourning After*)

A Three-Phase Approach

1. *Shock.* This is a period of temporary numbness.
2. *Suffering and disorganization.* Suffering can take many forms—anger, depression, guilt, loneliness, a feeling of having been abandoned, denial. The changes in our life brought on by the death of a loved one cause us to feel disorganized.
3. *Aftershocks and reorganization.* We recognize our new needs and begin to act on them. Sudden reminders of the loss, such as the anniversary of the death, may cause aftershocks.

(Summarized from Judy Tatelbaum, *The Courage to Grieve*)

Simon said nothing. He was looking down. "Simon," Father George tried again, "your envelope means a lot to you. I think it might even be a kind of lifeline for you. You don't have to take it out again, but I do think it might help you to tell us something about it." Simon didn't look up. After a strained silence, he said, "Thursday."

Simon's outburst allowed the group to witness an important part of grieving—confused rage about God. As a result, the others felt safer in admitting their own mixed feelings toward God. With the exception of Simon and Dawna, everyone went on to talk about the funerals they had attended, about what had brought on the tears, the questions, the anger. The experiences of which they spoke were bittersweet.

They had heard the proclamations of faith, God's promise of everlasting life. They had wanted to believe, to trust, to hope. But all they had felt was sorrow, rage, and despair. They were confused by the conflict of their own inner forces.

The confusion and conflict were seen most clearly in Keisha's situation. Following the car accident she had spent a week in the hospital.

"It was so hard to lie there in the hospital when almost the whole school was at Matthew's funeral. It's not that I felt like praying, but I wanted to be there with everybody else. When they told me that Nicole was dead, I just knew I had to go to her funeral. My doctor said it would be too soon for me, but I went anyway. It was so hard getting around in a wheelchair. I used to get from one end of the basketball court to the other in about two seconds. But after the accident, it hurt to move, even a little. But you know, being at Nicole's funeral was easier than missing Matthew's."

"But how could that be?" Simon couldn't resist voicing his question.

"I was mixed up about God, and mad, just like you. But I needed to hear those things about God being good and about there being a heaven. I needed to see all those other sad faces. And I even needed to see the coffin. Somehow the funeral helped my feelings come out. It helped me say good-bye. But you know what else? It seemed like all those people—even though they looked so weak and sad—looked strong together. I felt stronger when I left the church than when I first came in."

Father George easily identified with his students' struggle to understand how God could permit death and still be considered good. They needed to know that their beloved dead were in the arms of a loving God. They needed reassurance that no suffering in this life can outweigh the happiness of the next. It had taken Father George a lot of years, but finally he understood that not having an answer does not mean there is no answer.

Father George's Faith

Father George picked up his Bible. "I want to read you the line that got me through my father's funeral. 'The sufferings we now endure bear no comparison with the glory, as yet unrevealed, which is in store for us'" (Romans 8:18). Father George was imagining Charles, his father, in heaven. He was imagining his father free of the oppression of Alzheimer's—making sense again, recognizing his son again.

Everyone was looking at Father George. He seemed to be radiating peace and hope. Even Simon noticed it. Ms. Shields read aloud:

> It is our certain faith that Jesus Christ was raised from the dead. Grant that through this mystery, your servant, Charles Freedon, who has gone to be in Christ, may share in the joy of his Resurrection.

Father George leaned back in his chair. His eyes were wet and shining. "I know that all of you are hurting. I know how it feels to be at a funeral, raging inside. And believe me, I know how it feels to hate God. Day after day, at the hospital, I blasted away at God for not bringing my father back from Alzheimer's. The hurt is real. But the hope is also real. Even if it makes no sense to you at this moment, I just want you to know that right now I see my dad in heaven. And it feels great."

Ms. Shields was thinking about Father George's vision of his dad in heaven and how that vision had come into being. She understood that God has mysterious, often secret, ways of helping people discover the truth about things. Dawna, Sarah, Simon, and Keisha, though still searching, knew that there was something vital and powerfully mysterious at work in them—at work even in death.

Just before Tuesday's session ended, Sarah spoke: "My dad is mad at me now, about the letter I wrote him. He said I expect too much out of life. He said I should be glad I have a roof over my head. I should know that all his hard work is to provide for me." For a third time since the session had begun, fragile feelings of hope and reassurance were disrupted.

In the few remaining minutes there was time only for a brief response to Sarah. Ms. Shields reassured Sarah that writing her letter had been a good thing, an honest act of love. Sarah's father's reaction, she suggested, was his way of dealing with death: Don't hope for too much—and be glad of what you haven't yet lost.

The group left at five, and Sarah stayed to talk to Ms. Shields. Part of love is accepting the other's needs and limits, the inevitable disappointments of any relationship. By the time Sarah was ready to leave, she was able to say this much: "I guess grieving isn't just about taking care of myself and my own needs. I have to understand Dad's needs as well. But I'm glad I told him the truth. He has to know how *I* feel, too."

Simon's Courage

On Thursday, Simon's black backpack was not in its usual spot beside his chair. He was holding it in his lap. Dawna noticed that Simon seemed angry. Simon's experience of Sash's funeral had been one of unremitting gloom. Unlike Keisha, he had seen no light piercing the darkness. With Simon's anger almost palpable, Dawna's anxiety rose. She didn't know that his anger was rooted in having to face his own pain—and Sash's.

A Secret, Spoken

Usually the group session began with a few minutes of quiet time. Each person was to let surface any thoughts, feelings, or unanswered questions. But this day was different. Simon spoke at the very beginning.

"I'm not going to show you the envelope. I'm not telling you what's in it. I just want to say one thing. Sash was my twin. He committed suicide. He overdosed on barbiturates. No one knows where he got them. I hated the funeral. Stupid flowers and singing. I haven't told my family, but Sash left a suicide note. It was under my pillow the morning we found him." Simon's sentences were short and quick, like stabs in the dark.

Simon's sentences were like stabs in the dark.

Simon folded his arms across his backpack. It was as if he were holding something, almost as if he wanted to give it comfort. Dawna was still nervous about Simon's anger, but anxiety now mixed with sympathy as she watched his face tighten and his eyes narrow. Dawna could tell he was afraid he would cry in front of the group.

He was holding that backpack as if it were a baby. Watching him, Dawna ached to hold Mary in her arms. Dawna pulled the cushion from under her elbow and placed it in her lap. It was a fuzzy, soft, coral-colored cushion. Dawna and Simon sat side by side, one holding a backpack and the other a cushion, both aching to be comforted.

Dawna was sure that if Simon cried or screamed, she would too.

The Envelope

Simon did not scream. Inside, though, he was experiencing a rapid succession of thoughts and feelings: reliving the funeral, remembering his last conversation with Sash, thinking about what was in the envelope. Outwardly, he sat like stone.

1
The final conversations with a loved one before his or her death take on special meaning for the grief-stricken, especially in the case of sudden, unexpected death. What reasons might be behind this?

After a while, Simon slowly unzipped his backpack. One by one he lifted his textbooks out of the bag. When the bag lay limp on the table, Simon gingerly pulled out the last of the bag's contents: the envelope. The tape had been cut, and the envelope was already ripped open.

Simon's initial statement that the envelope's contents would not be revealed had been more of an instruction for himself than a pronouncement to the group. He really had not intended to take the envelope out of the bag. However, not only was the envelope out of the bag, but Simon was now pulling something out of the envelope. His hands were shaking. He felt embarrassed about the trembling, but couldn't make it stop. He hoped that no one would notice, but everyone did.

In his hand, Simon held a folded piece of mauve paper. It was the same paper Father George had distributed in the fifth group meeting. On it were the words Jesus had spoken the night before his own death: "'My heart is ready to break with grief. Stop here, and stay awake with me.'"

Simon did not unfold the mauve paper, but placed it with great care on the edge of the table, directly in front of him. Then Simon pulled out a second folded piece of paper, this one white. Simon did not unfold this one either. He placed the white one beside the mauve one on the table, directly in front of him.

The empty backpack slipped to the floor, but Simon did not notice. His attention was fixed entirely on the two pieces of paper. They were identical, except in color. He and Sash had been like that—identical, except for their hairstyles. Simon and Sash. Sash and Simon. Twins. Side-by-side. Always together.

It was much too painful for Simon to tell the group about the white paper and the dark secret it bore. The white one was Sash's suicide note, the one Simon had found under his pillow the day Sash died. When Simon read Sash's note, he felt as if he were being torn apart. In the note, Sash had begged Simon to commit suicide too.

In the last few months leading up to his death, Sash had found life increasingly unbearable. But Sash had kept his anguish to himself; he and Simon were totally alike in their dread of self-disclosure. Sadly, Sash didn't live long enough to search out the roots of his problems. Suicide ended any possibilities there might have been for Sash to rise above his fears, come to terms with himself, and learn to enjoy life.

Sash had felt alone in life, except for Simon. He wanted Simon to follow him into death.

Despite his longing to respond to Sash's dying plea, Simon could not make a deliberate and conscious choice to bring about his own death. Simon suffered a double agony: his awareness, which had come too late, of Sash's pain, and his realization that he must remain separated from Sash.

Finally Simon wanted to speak aloud. He slowly unfolded the mauve paper. His voice was low: "I wrote Sash a note on this paper. I want you to hear it." Until now, Simon's sentences had been short and quick, like controlled cries of pain. What he said now came out quite differently, in a voice the group had not heard before. His words were like deep sighs, coming straight from his heart. Softly, he read: "Dear Sash. I have decided to live for both of us now." Simon paused, then finished: "I love you, Sash. Simon."

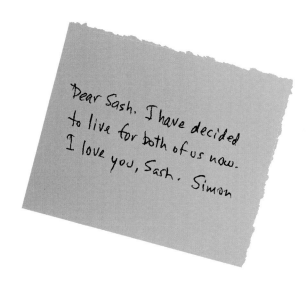

Simon's Salvation

Simon had always been secretly interested in religion and Jesus, but that interest had been mixed with skepticism. Simon's skepticism had moved into cynicism since Sash's suicide. But something was beginning to change in Simon. He could understand Jesus' plea not to be left alone. In that plea, Jesus seemed real to Simon.

Simon cried soundlessly. He was staring at the two unfolded pieces of paper on the table. All the while Simon had been speaking, Dawna had held her cushion, cradling it in her arms like a lost child. Her tears poured out.

Keisha was thinking that Simon's guilt might have been an even heavier burden than hers. Simon's accusations against God resonated with her own. That Thursday afternoon at five o'clock, the four students and two staff members were exhausted. But the load each carried seemed a little lighter.

2
Expressing anger toward God is healthy. Anger is a God-given gift, a powerful force rising from the most primal depths of the human person. Rage-filled prayer can bring us into radical intimacy with God. Deep-rooted healing can follow. Have you ever had an experience of anger, at God or at another person, that helped you to know God, yourself, or that other person better?

Week 5: A "Funeral" for Baby Mary

As Tuesday's session began, the air in the room was heavy with guilt. Simon had made a great deal of progress, but the story inside the envelope was unfinished. Today, though, Dawna's needs would come to the foreground.

As usual, the session began with the precious belongings being placed on the coffee table. Simon's mauve and white papers were there, though he had placed them inside a new envelope, which he had sealed. Dawna's baby's pacifier was there. Dawna picked it up at the beginning of the session.

"Mary needs a funeral," she whispered, her eyes on the pacifier. Sarah understood. She was remembering the seemingly endless funeral procession that had led her grandmother's casket to the altar last November. She had hated every step, but that funeral had been filled with unexpected treasures: her father's gaze into her soul, his reaching out and shaking Mike's hand, her brother's first voluntary hug, the bright flame over Uncle Philip's head, Corey's little hand wrapped around her own, the sounds of song piercing the dark clouds of her grief.

"Could we have a funeral for Mary here at school?" Sarah asked the question that seemed to be rising from the whole group. Despite Simon's ambivalence and Keisha's impression that she was too guilty to be anywhere near God, everyone wanted to have a service for the baby who had never been born. The remainder of the session was spent planning.

Neither Father George nor Ms. Shields considered this a disruption to their plans. They knew that adjustment based on individual needs was an essential part of the grieving process. Both knew that the primary grieving agenda must come not from the leaders but from the needs, feelings, and rhythms of the mourners themselves. The pathways of grieving are unique to each group and person.

"Light Shone in the Darkness"

On Thursday, seven candles stood burning on the altar of Saint Monica's chapel. Around the altar stood six mourners.

A tall blue candle burned for Ms. Shields's brother, David. A white candle burned for Sarah's grandmother; at its base was a red rose held in place with a fine gold cord. In-

side a dark blue cracked glass, a flame burned for Simon's twin. Keisha's two matching candles in tall gold candlesticks had been lit for Matthew and Nicole. Father George's old brass holder, brought from his office, now held a new white candle. In the center of the altar, surrounded by the others, Dawna had placed a silver dish bearing a tiny heart-shaped pink candle.

Father George and Ms. Shields had helped the group to plan a simple prayer service. It opened with a blessing, then a reading:

> "Yahweh called me when I was in the womb,
> before my birth he had pronounced my name.
>
> . . . .
> I shall not forget you.
> Look, I have engraved you on the palms of my hands."
> (Isaiah 49:1,15–16)

Ms. Shields followed with a solemn assertion: "Mary is safe with God. God calls her by name. She is loved."

Dawna began to pray, but not out loud.

Dawna was thinking of all the things Mary would never experience. Mary would never know how it felt to lose someone. She would never attend a funeral. Mary would never go through the grief Dawna was now going through. But Dawna wasn't thinking how fortunate Mary was. It hurt her to know that Mary would never hold anyone's hand, never be hugged, never be kissed, never fall in love. Dawna's guilt was heavy. Because of it, the hope-filled words of Isaiah could not penetrate her soul.

Ms. Shields continued: "We too are safely held in God's love, being sheltered, protected, and made well.

"My steadfast love shall not depart from you,

. . . .

O afflicted one, storm-tossed, and not comforted,
I am about to set your stones in antimony,
and lay your foundations with sapphires.
I will make your pinnacles of rubies,
your gates of jewels,
and all your walls of precious stones."

(Isaiah 54:10–12)

Ms. Shields explained that antimony is a kind of crystal with a bluish white luster, used chiefly for its strength. Sapphires, she said, are precious stones—bright blue, clear, and transparent. Rubies are a deep, glowing red gem. Isaiah's vision was one of God honoring, cherishing, and strengthening the beloved.

At that moment, the Isaiah passage sparked something in Dawna: an echo of jewels, of beauty, of steadfast love. Dawna began to pray, but not out loud: "God, I'm not sure what heaven is. But I know that Mary must be in heaven. She never did anything wrong. I don't know if it's okay for me to ask you for anything, but could someone hold her hand in heaven?"

Sarah saw the tears stream from Dawna's eyes. Sarah reached for the red rose she had tied to her candle. She undid its gold cord. With great care, she took the rose and placed it in the silver dish, beside the heart-shaped candle Dawna had lit for her unborn child.

Dawna, who always stood ramrod straight and exulted in her self-sufficiency, now bent a little. She leaned against Sarah.

Dawna felt weak. And for the first time in months, Sarah felt strong.

Simon hadn't taken his eyes off the cracked blue glass. He had deliberately chosen a broken candleholder. Simon and Sash were both broken. The flame was difficult to see through the heavy blue. Simon was thinking that Sash was like that dark flame—hidden now and gone from reach, but still there somewhere.

Simon's hand was in his pocket. He was holding Sash's suicide note and his own letter to Sash, together. Looking up, Simon noticed Dawna leaning against Sarah. He wished he could lean like that.

For a long time, the mourners stood in silence around the altar as the candles burned. Then Dawna's heart-shaped candle, tiny as it was, went out. Keisha gasped, "I'm so sorry." Keisha's gasp was an expression of her empathy for Dawna. Her apology was an expression of repentance. Empathy had opened a door in Keisha. Her remorse over her own failures came out. With remorse came the first stirrings of peace.

Dawna bent low over the candle, a tiny puff of smoke rising up from it. "Good-bye," she said.

At the start of funeral week, Father George had suggested to the group that saying good-bye is part of recognizing and accepting our loss. We may say good-bye all at once or

3
Those who are grief-stricken should not be left to stand alone. When we are most vulnerable, most in touch with the intensities of life and death, we need one another most of all. If Simon were to lean on someone, do you think his ability to do grief-work would be enhanced or diminished? Why?

gradually. Saying good-bye frees us from an unhealthy clinging to, and preoccupation with, the past. Paradoxically, it also sets us free to love more fully. Once we have said good-bye, we can love those who have died in a more profound way, a way based not on flesh and blood, but on Christ alone. Father George had explained, "Jesus Christ transcends the grave; in him, our love knows no bounds."

When Dawna whispered, "Good-bye," Father George sensed that she had taken a big step into healing.

Ms. Shields opened a notebook and read aloud:

Shining vermilion
towered over the steep gray rock,
yellows and fire-reds
shot out among the dark evergreens
and all lay covered in copper-soft blushes
with orange brilliantly intense.

Fall had come to the trees
And I thought perhaps this might be the first autumn I
    had ever seen.
How I wished to bask there forever.

O slender leaves, you bearers of beauty,
gather up your strength,
resist with all your might the harsh winds
assembling on the far horizon.
How I dread seeing you torn apart.
O fragile creatures, do not fall from the trees!

But I sat.
And I became quiet.
And the leaves began to fall softly, soundlessly.
Without objection they floated down to the green bed
    waiting below.
And I watched as the branches slowly became bare
and the bed quickly layered
with dying treasures.

But I was surprised.
I had not known that such a fall could be so soft.
I had not expected the quiet, nor the wind's tender
    caress.
I had not imagined that peace would flow in with the
    dying.
And I turned toward winter.
"Come, my love" was all I heard.

Mary's funeral came to a close.

Week 6:
Where Are We Going?

Looking Inward

Simon, Dawna, Keisha, and Sarah were surprised at their own disappointment that the Grief Support Group sessions were drawing to a close. The six weeks, which had appeared insurmountable and unending at the outset, now seemed fleeting. This little knot of mourners had found a bond in their shared suffering. They had learned that no one should grieve alone. It had been a comfort to belong to such a group.

The four students were beginning to learn what Ms. Shields and Father George had known for a long time—that grieving, though difficult, is as essential to human living as is water or air or food.

The final week was devoted to assessment, not with tests and grades, but with gentle, honest, inward-looking reflection. Its purpose was to discern the next step in the grieving process for each of the four young mourners. This careful discernment was intended to help the students plan what each of them might need after the group sessions ended.

A Rose with Thorns

It was early June. Sarah's grandmother's rose garden had just begun to bloom, even without Martha Spencer's continued care. That sparked something in Sarah—an unexpected delight in the discovery that to be abandoned is not necessarily to die, that life forces are at work even when all appears lost. After Sarah had brought a rose to school for Mary's prayer service, Ms. Shields asked her to bring another for this next-to-last meeting. "Make sure it has a lot of thorns," Ms. Shields requested. Sarah thought she knew why.

Sarah placed the rose in a vase on the coffee table. The rose was almost iridescent, a sort of carmine pink under an orange wash. Nearby was the pill bottle Ms. Shields had brought, the photograph of Matthew and Nicole, Father George's prayer book, the baby's pacifier, and Simon's sealed envelope. Sarah's gold ring was not on the table; she was wearing it. She no longer took it from her finger.

Sarah told the others that the rose in the vase was called a Tropicana. Because of its scent, the Tropicana had been her grandmother's favorite. That scent reminded Sarah of cutting

Memories evoked by the five senses are often more vivid than those brought on by thought. For example, the taste of a certain breakfast food may evoke memories of childhood. Which of your senses bring out the strongest memories?

roses with her grandmother in Junes gone by. With the scent of this particular rose, Sarah could almost feel as she once had, standing with her grandmother in the rose garden.

Placed into Your Hands

Ms. Shields reached across the table of precious belongings and lifted the Tropicana rose out of its vase. Reverently, she placed it in Sarah's hands. Then Ms. Shields spoke to the group.

"This afternoon, Sarah's rose will be passed to each of us. When the rose comes to you, take a few minutes to really look at it. Notice not only its color and fragrance and beauty, but its thorns. Touch them and see how sharp they are. As you hold the rose, think about what has been placed into your life because of death—both what's painful and what's beautiful, what's visible and what's still hidden, what's healing and what's still hurting, what's strong and what's weak. Speak out loud if you want to. Or just stay quiet, with the rose in your hands."

Sarah held the rose for a long time. The rebirth of the rose garden in the spring following her grandmother's death had given Sarah new hope. More and more, Sarah was living out of the belief that her grandmother's life—like the rose garden—continued. Death did not end life, it changed it.

For a second, she deliberately pushed one of the thorns into the palm of her hand. She wanted to feel the thorn's tiny stab. Then she said: "I want to feel the pain. Somehow the pain makes me feel as if I'm still connected with my grandmother."

Sarah was glad to think that the sadness seemed permanently rooted in her. Father George spoke: "Sarah, it's good to stay connected with the ones we love. And as long as I live, I don't think my own pain over my dad's death will ever be completely gone. But it's dangerous to deliberately try to hold on to the pain. What we need to hold on to is the love—that way we can gradually let go of the pain."

Sarah thought she understood. But it would be scary to let go of the pain. Was her love strong enough to sustain her? She didn't know. Sarah passed the rose to Keisha.

A few weeks ago, Keisha could not have held that rose. The sharp thorns would have brought out her guilt, reminding her of the punishment she felt she deserved. But today Keisha was able not only to hold the rose, but also to bear what still remained of her guilt. As she lowered her head and breathed in the flower's scent, her long dark hair almost hid the rose from the group's sight.

Keisha was remembering the red rose Sarah had placed in the dish holding Dawna's heart-shaped candle. As she held the rose, she told the group what had happened to her during that service for Mary. Keisha explained that when Mary's tiny candle had gone out, her own guilt feelings were the worst she'd ever felt. That's why she had gasped out loud. "I was so embarrassed to lose control like that, but, you know, it made me feel better. After that, the guilt feelings weren't as bad. It was a relief to say, 'I'm sorry,' and to say it out loud."

"Keisha, accepting your guilt is a big part of healing, and so is openly expressing your remorse. One day you'll be free of this guilt." Simon listened carefully as Ms. Shields spoke to Keisha. He couldn't imagine being free of his guilt.

Keisha passed the rose to Father George.

"Roses have always been mysterious to me. The way the petals are packed in so tightly. I love to watch a rose open. When I think of my dad now, I think he might be like this rose—beginning to open. I think of everything that's so good in him, coming out again. My dad, no longer a prisoner of Alzheimer's. I wish I could see him for myself." His brow furrowed slightly, then relaxed. He held out the rose to Simon.

Simon shook his head. "I don't want it."

Father George paused. Then, instead, he offered the rose to Dawna. She took it. She stroked its soft petals as if she were stroking a baby's face. She thought about Mary every day and sometimes dreamed about her at night. She rubbed her finger under the end of the stem, where it had been cut off. Dawna's remorse was still a heavy burden, as was her sense of loss. Dawna couldn't help thinking that in a day or two, this flower would be withered and dead. And there would be nothing anyone could do to stop it from dying.

She returned it quickly to its water in the vase.

After a few minutes, Ms. Shields picked up not just the rose, but the whole vase. Intuitively she sensed it would be too painful for Dawna to see the rose taken from the water again.

Ms. Shields spoke: "Dawna, I'm glad the rose is back in the vase. It's good to see it in water again. Although David is not physically present anymore, I know he's being held somehow, just like the rose is held in this vase of water.

> Keisha could bear what remained of her guilt.

Somewhere he's safe, being taken care of. I really do believe that. But I've learned a lot since David's death. I don't expect life to be fair anymore, at least not by human standards. God allows each person his or her own unique measure of blessings and crosses. There's no point comparing what I have with what somebody else has. I must live whatever comes my way—with faith and hope."

A Mysterious Presence

The conversation paused for a moment. Keisha picked up the photo of Nicole and Matthew, then put it down and took a breath. "Can I say something? It's a bit weird, so I don't know if it's okay to talk about it."

Ms. Shields nodded. "Of course it's okay, Keisha. Go ahead."

"It was last Friday night—the day after Mary's funeral. I was in my room, up late. I couldn't make myself do anything, but I didn't want to just do nothing, so I sat down at my desk to look at my biology homework. All of a sudden it felt like someone was in the room with me, like Nicole was there and we were doing homework together the way we used to—with a lot more laughing and talking about guys and stuff than real homework. I turned around, and of course I was alone, but it still felt like Nicole was there. I could almost smell her perfume. But I wasn't scared. What was really weird was that I felt good. Then I went to sleep and didn't wake up for hours."

Father George spoke next. "I think experiences like that happen to a lot of us, though sometimes we're not as attuned to them as you apparently were. A few years after my dad died, for example, I was walking along a street in a part of the city I hadn't been in for a long time, and I started thinking of him. That's not unusual, but I was thinking specifically about when I was seven or eight years old and he and I would walk on city streets. Then I realized where I was— across the street from the building he worked in when I was a child. It was hardly recognizable, all refurbished, but it was the place. When I was a kid my dad would take me with him on weekends; he'd work some overtime in his office while I did homework or puzzles on the floor. It all came back, like it had just happened yesterday."

"The people that we love become very strong presences in our life," said Ms. Shields. "And when they have died, it's very common to feel that we are in contact with them. Not the Hollywood movie kind of contact, where someone's ghost walks in and tells you how to live your life or, worse

yet, makes your life miserable. But the kind of presence described by both Keisha and Father George."

In spite of himself, Simon spoke: "It could be just an illusion or a hallucination." Simon, who felt the presence of his brother in his mind and heart almost constantly, secretly wished for a logical explanation.

"Grieving is a stressful process," said Father George, "and it *is* possible for the mind to play tricks on us. We have to remember that. But the Catholic church teaches that the church itself is a communion, or community, of saints. That means that the church consists of all who believe, living or dead. The living and the dead are united in Christ. The living are connected to the dead through prayer. Our loved ones who have died are still our loved ones. And the love remains with us, sometimes in the background, sometimes in the foreground."

Keisha felt affirmed but still a bit confused. "I didn't tell anyone else about this," she admitted. "I didn't know if I should be scared, happy, or just forget it."

Ms. Shields suggested that Keisha simply accept the experience. She shouldn't make too much of it, nor should she dismiss it entirely. It was just one of the many aspects of her healing journey. "Some things we'll never be able to fully explain or understand," said Ms. Shields. "But it's less important to understand everything than it is to trust God, especially with the things we don't understand."

Continuing, on Gold-Edged Pages

The remainder of Tuesday's session was spent helping the group members to better identify their hurts and their hopes, the obstacles and the challenges still lying ahead of them on their paths of grief.

Simon had felt fearful of touching the rose. He had no intention of speaking aloud about his feelings. Inside, he conceded that it was probably good for him to allow himself to feel the hurt, but he didn't feel comfortable letting the group see very much of his inner self. He was to feel more at ease doing the private journaling exercise with which the session would end.

Father George placed four hard-covered journals on the table. Each journal was different, but Keisha was delighted to see that all of them had gold-edged pages. Gold had become, for her, a sign of hope. Each person took a book and wrote two inscriptions inside. The first was his or her name, and the other was the name of the loved one who had died. Writing in a journal was to be part of the process by which these mourners would remain in loving communion with their dead. At the same time, journal writing would help the mourners free themselves to enter more deeply into other loving relationships. And the book was a place to talk to God and write down feelings and questions about God.

Ms. Shields and Father George showed the students their own current journals, each speaking of the therapeutic value of writing. They both had been keeping journals for years. Seeing those two worn-looking books helped the students; they had learned to trust the experience of their two leaders.

Entries could be made daily, beginning today. What was written was to remain private. No rules were given about what should or should not be recorded in the journals. The only other instruction was that keeping the journals should be a conscious way of continuing the grieving process. After two weeks of journal writing, each student would have a one-to-one talk with Ms. Shields or Father George. Together they would decide what was needed for continued healing and growth.

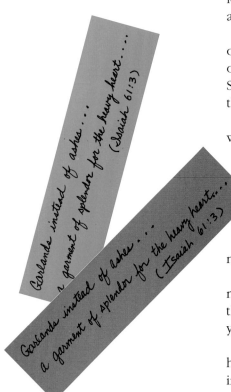

On Tuesday, at ten minutes to five, the gold-edged journals were opened to page 1. As the six mourners entered their first reflections, they were thinking about what might yet lie ahead of them.

Father George's journal fell shut in his lap. Although he had often helped people who were grieving, he always felt inadequate in the face of others' grief. At a certain point, despite giving all he had to give, Father George knew that he had to entrust his students' lives into God's hands. He had to trust that God would go with them where he could not, just as he had trusted God with his own father.

Everyone else was writing. Quietly, and without drawing attention to himself, Father George reached across the coffee table to place a bookmark beside each person. On each bookmark, he had written,

Garlands instead of ashes . . .
a garment of splendour for the heavy heart. . . .

(Isaiah 61:3)

In the silence of his soul, Father George asked God to lead his students into increased healing and peace. Simon read what was on his bookmark. Then he looked up. Father George saw something he had not seen before. In Simon's eyes was the barest hint of a smile.

Verbal Garlands

Just before five o'clock, the group was given a special assignment. They were asked to bring "verbal garlands" with them to Thursday's closing session. These verbal garlands were to be heartfelt thank-yous, spoken aloud. Each person would thank each of the others for her or his unique contributions to the group.

That night, Dawna took out her journal just before going to bed. In small letters at the bottom of the first page, she wrote, "From now on I'm going to call my baby Mary Rose." That's all Dawna wrote. She wasn't feeling well; she hoped sleep would help.

Plans for Peace

Thursday had come, the day of the last session. Ms. Shields couldn't resist bringing something chocolate. The precious belongings had been taken home, leaving the coffee table empty. At each person's usual spot, Ms. Shields placed a chocolate fudge truffle. Each chocolate treasure was held in a tiny gold-foil cup.

After everyone had gathered, Ms. Shields spoke: "'My plans for you are peace and not disaster' (Jeremiah 29:11). This is what God tells us. When I saw my brother dead, I did not trust God's promise. I thought my agony would never end. I did not believe that God had any intention of bringing me peace. I know differently now, even though I still miss David very much."

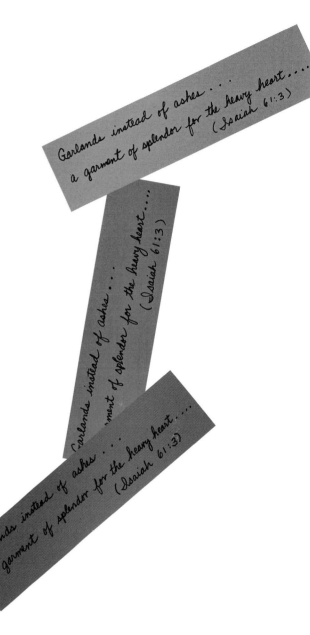

Picking up one of the gold-foil cups, Ms. Shields continued: "I want you to have these chocolate truffles not just because I love chocolate, but because they are a sign of celebration. Good things will come from all this hurting. I know we haven't finished dealing with all our confusion and hostility and hurt, but that doesn't mean we can't have a taste of something good right now. So let's celebrate. Let's eat some chocolate!" Everyone smiled.

Love Must Always Have the Victory

The room was peaceful with the sounds of enjoyment. Simon and Keisha were still licking their fingers when Father George gave the first verbal garland. "Simon," he said, "I really admire your courage. It's no small challenge to be the only guy in a group of girls, and you've never missed a session. You've always been honest. I have benefited from your being in this group. Thank you." As Simon carefully stacked the empty gold cups into a single neat pile, Father George noticed the return of that faint smile. Simon was touched by Father George's statement.

Many verbal garlands followed, each like a bouquet of flowers. Ms. Shields thanked Sarah not only for the roses, but for her love of the roses. The tender care with which Sarah handled her grandmother's roses made Ms. Shields feel somehow cared for as well, and that was such a good feeling.

Sarah thanked each person. She spoke most about Keisha's perseverance. Sarah knew how hard it was for Keisha to continue with the group after Jerome had dropped out. Sarah understood all too well the experience of being abandoned. She knew how horrible it felt to be left behind. She thanked Keisha for staying.

Dawna thanked Father George for inviting her to join the group. Although it had been difficult, the group had given Dawna a lot of help. After giving individual garlands to each member, she added: "Best of all was the prayer service for my baby. I couldn't believe how much it hurt to see Mary Rose's candle go out, but the other candles kept burning all around it. If that little candle had gone out in the dark all by itself, I couldn't have taken it."

"You put Rose in her name?" Sarah had turned to speak to Dawna. "It sounds so pretty like that."

"It's because God makes rosebuds bloom into roses," Dawna answered. "It was like I cut off a rosebud before it ever had a chance to grow." Inside, where only God could hear, Dawna added, "God, I'll always call her Mary Rose because I'll always hope that you can help the rosebud become a rose."

Keisha gave garlands of gratitude to each group member. She especially thanked Ms. Shields and Father George, because they always let the students know that they, the teachers, were just as much a part of the group as the rest of them. "You both took a big risk with us. You knew that talking with a bunch of grieving students could bring out your own grief. I think that's what compassion is. Thank you."

Simon still hated speaking out loud. He hated calling attention to himself. And Father George had hit the nail on the head: it was particularly difficult for him to be the only male in a group of females. However, as he witnessed this exchange of garlands—this expression of love—he wanted to give some garlands of his own.

Among Simon's garlands was one for Dawna. He couldn't bring himself to look her in the eyes as he spoke. Still, he managed to say: "Dawna, this sounds strange, but I saw you lean on Sarah when Mary's candle went out. You looked kind of weak, but you didn't cover that up. I thought leaning on people was bad, but now I'm not so sure. I think I am starting to see it differently. Thanks."

Simon had another part to his verbal garland, but he wasn't able to say it out loud. He was remembering the day he couldn't keep from crying over the mauve and white letters. Although he had resisted turning his head to look at her, he knew that Dawna was crying with him. That had made such a difference. He had noticed, too, how Dawna had pulled a cushion into her lap. It had consoled Simon to see Dawna cuddling that cushion. He himself had ached to touch something or someone, but he could not move. Somehow Dawna had done all the things he himself had needed to do but couldn't.

Still looking down, Simon did not see Dawna's face as he spoke. But the others saw. She was radiant. She really did look like someone who had just received a garland of flowers. Dawna moved closer to Simon and—lightly, tentatively—touched his shoulder. "I like you," she said.

Dawna's touch and her whispered "I like you" reached down into the very root of Simon's being, right down into the place where he had felt the worst pain. Simon was so overwhelmed that he could not look at Dawna. But he knew that Dawna was smiling.

And so was Simon.

The trap is broken, and we have escaped.
Our help is in the name of the LORD,
maker of heaven and earth.

(Psalm 124:7–8)

10
Arise, My Love

*A*lleluia, the Great Storm is over.
Lift up your wings and fly.

—*Bob Franke*

The Finding of the Lost

A Cry for Help

Almost a year had passed since the Grief Support Group had finished. It was the end of the day, and Father George was checking for messages on his voice mail. There was just one: "Father George, I had no one else to call but you. I'm dying, I'm really dying. I'm so afraid to face God. Can you please, please call me? It's 777-7000, room 309."

The voice was female, definitely familiar, and frail. He recognized the number as that of Centenary Hospital. He dialed and asked for room 309. The phone rang in room 309. The same voice answered with a thin, "Hello." Father George realized, with surprise, who was speaking to him. It was someone who had dropped out of sight almost a year before.

"Hello, Dawna—it's Father George. . . . Dawna, what's wrong?"

Dawna started to cry. She told her story in a broken voice, starting with how rough the summer had been after the Grief Support Group had ended. Dawna's father had remarried. He had all but stopped calling her. Dawna's mother had a new boyfriend, Vin. Vin was an alcoholic and a pipe dreamer. Dawna did not trust him. She felt unsafe around him. Dawna got herself a part-time job cleaning up at a burger place. She came home as little as possible.

Finally, in mid-August, Dawna's mother announced: "Vin's taking us to Florida to start over. Get packing." Dawna packed, but she had no intention of going with them. When

moving day came, Dawna was nowhere to be found. Her mother and Vin left anyway.

Dawna was left with nothing but three cardboard boxes of her belongings. She moved into an abandoned building in a low-rent section of town. She ate what she could scrounge or steal. Sometimes her boss gave her leftover burgers. Dawna never went back to school. She kept entirely to herself, not wanting anyone—not her father, not Father George, not Simon, Keisha, or Sarah—to find out that her life had completely fallen apart.

The school contacted Dawna's father to say she was missing. Her mother had left no forwarding address. Early in the school year, her father came to town for a week. He asked questions, went to the police, looked around, but found no evidence of either his daughter or his ex-wife. With his new family needing him back home, he felt he had no choice but to leave the matter to the police.

Having investigated the situation, the police could only conclude that Dawna was with her mother. No crime other than truancy had been committed, so they saw nothing further to be done. The faculty and staff of Saint Monica's did not have the resources to search further, and it was reasonable to assume that Dawna had left with her mother. Her name was dropped from the enrollment.

Meanwhile, the winter was bitter. To keep warm, Dawna worked extra unpaid hours or just hung around in the kitchen at work. Several times during the winter she had to move out of one abandoned building into another. The city was systematically demolishing unsafe buildings in her section of town. Other homeless people lived nearby, but she spoke to none of them. She wanted no one to know her story. In fact, she wanted to cease to exist altogether.

Dawna had never regained full strength following the abortion. Toward the end of the winter, she was feeling more ill than usual. She knew something was wrong, but she sought no treatment. She told herself it was just a really bad cold. But it wasn't a cold.

At work, she covered up her symptoms as much as she could, but her condition worsened. She became disoriented. One day she collapsed in the kitchen. Her boss called an ambulance, and Dawna was taken to Centenary Hospital.

Dawna was facing death—alone.

At the hospital Dawna learned that she had bacterial pneumonia. Because of her debilitated condition in recent months, the disease was even more destructive than usual. The doctors attempted to treat her, but Dawna had already passed the point at which treatment could save her.

As Dawna finished speaking, Father George felt numb. The details of her past year shocked him. Dawna, having mourned the loss of a child, was herself little more than a child. Now she was facing death—alone.

Dawna's voice became a little stronger over the phone line. "Father, a long time ago I gave you a sand picture. My dad gave it to me for my birthday when I was little. I loved the blues and pinks. It was always changing. I could always make a new picture in it, just by tilting it a little. I liked that. I always thought of it as being filled with a million pictures of hope. I never told you it was from me because I didn't know if it was right to give someone a used gift." Suddenly Dawna's voice broke. "But Father, I don't have any hope anymore." She was sobbing.

"Listen, Sweetheart, I'll be there within an hour." And he hung up. Father George rarely addressed students—or anyone else, for that matter—as Sweetheart. In fact, he was not even conscious of what he had said. But Dawna was. As she hung up, she felt as if she had been hugged.

Burdened and Dying

Father George swept up the sand picture off his top shelf and rushed out. Centenary Hospital was on the far side of town, traffic would be heavy, and he had a purchase to make: white tissue paper and a gold ribbon and bow.

Each time he was stopped at a red light, he blamed himself: "Why wasn't I able to do more for Dawna when she was still at school?"

When Father George arrived at room 309, Dawna was sleeping. His heart was heavy as he looked down at this child dying among strangers. She looked small and forsaken in that clinical white bed. Her skin was ashen and her hair limp, with almost no curl left in it. Gone was the red lipstick from the rosebud lips. The only color in her face would have been the green of her eyes, but they were closed.

"Dear God, why has this happened?" Father George thought. "Hasn't she suffered enough already in her short life? A year ago I thought there was real hope for her. She had made her peace with Mary Rose, and new life was rising up in her. Oh, my God, what should I have done differently?" He quietly pulled out the package he had wrapped in white tissue paper with gold ribbon and a gold bow. It looked exactly as it had when Dawna had given it to him. Gently, he placed it beside her on the bed.

Then he sat down to wait, hoping she would awaken. Looking into the gaunt face of the dying Dawna, Father George felt like Jesus' mother must have felt at the foot of the cross. He recalled the Pietà, an ancient image of Jesus' mother holding her dead son in her arms. He sensed the excruciating pain of the Mother of God. He was as powerless to restore Dawna's life as the Blessed Mother had been to restore the life of Christ, for only God could raise the dead to life.

"Jesus Christ," he begged, "Help Dawna!"

1
To grieve is to feel powerless, to come face-to-face with our own utter dependence on God. Denial no longer works. We stand naked before God. The temptation in grief is to rebel against our own weakness, condemning the kind of life we have been given, moving into despair. The challenge in grief is to embrace the human condition and fall into the loving arms of God. Faced by your natural human weakness, do you tend to rebel against it or embrace it?

Pietà

A Poem by Rainer Maria Rilke

Now is my suffering complete as pain
unutterable fills my entire being.
I stare, am numb and rigid as a rock
is rigid to its very core.

Hard as I am, I do remember this:
you grew to boyhood—
. . . grew in height and strength,
you stood apart and overshadowed me,
became too great a sorrow, far beyond
the limits of my poor heart's understanding.

Now you lie, stilled in death, across my lap;
now I no longer can bring back your life
through birth.

Above: *Pietà of Kwangju* (circa 1980), by
Taeko Tomiyama.

Left: *Deploration of Christ* (1913), by Heinrich
Nauen.

Below left: *Lamentation, or Descent from the
Cross* (1944), by William H. Johnson.

Below: *Pietà* (1499), by Michelangelo
Buonarrotti.

Infinite Love

Dawna's eyes opened. With their flash of green, Father George felt a flutter of hope. He sat up in his chair. Her eyes fell on the white package with the gold bow. A questioning smile crept over her face.

"Open it," he said, smiling.

Dawna pulled on the gold ribbon, and the tissue fell away. "The sand picture!" she said softly. She hadn't the strength to pick it up, so she bumped it gently with her elbow. The rich blues and reds swirled softly inside their dark frame, revealing the merest hint of that beautiful rose-pink tinging the dark blues.

Shyly she asked, "Father, why are you giving it to me?"

"Remember what you said on the phone? This is a picture of hope—it's a million pictures of hope. I want you to have this now, Dawna. I always wondered who had given me such a great gift. The sand picture always gave me hope. It reminded me of God's love. That's what I want you to have now—hope and love.

"Dawna, on the phone you said that you were afraid to face God. Can you tell me why?"

Dawna turned her head away. She was crying again. Father George took her hand, and she turned back to him, her eyes dark with tears.

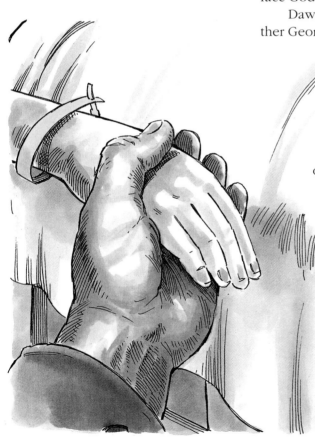

"Father, I'm going to be dead at the age of sixteen. That's a lot of years compared to what I gave Mary Rose. It still hurts so much. If I had kept her, I'd have someone to love now. God loves Mary Rose, but he doesn't love me! I'm scared of God!" Father George's strong hand closed over Dawna's.

"Dawna, can you feel your hand inside mine? Can you feel how much I care for you?" She nodded. "God's love is so much more than that. God's love for you is like this sand picture; you can shake it up a million times and still get a new picture. There's no end to it. God's love for you is like that. It never comes to an end."

"But Father, God's love is only for people who always do good. I didn't always do good. Mary Rose wasn't the only one I ever hurt; I did a lot of rotten things to my mom. I used to steal money out of her purse when she was drunk. I was so mad at her."

"Dawna, do you love Mary Rose?" She nodded. Her chin was trembling uncontrollably.

"Just close your eyes and feel yourself loving her." Dawna closed her eyes. Her hand, still inside Father George's, relaxed. "Dawna, you're feeling your own goodness—your own holiness—in your love for Mary Rose. God says, 'All who live in love live in me.' God has already forgiven your sins, Dawna. Let go of them. Feel God's arms around you."

Dawna opened her eyes, frightened and angry. "I can't!"

Father George fell silent. Dawna was helpless, and so was he. He took off his glasses and rubbed his eyes, praying in an almost inaudible voice, "'Glory be to him whose power, working in us, can do infinitely more than we can ask or imagine'" (Ephesians 3:20).

Father George had not expected her to be listening, but Dawna heard every word. In awe, she asked, "Father, did you say, 'more than we can imagine'?"

He looked up. "Infinitely, Dawna, infinitely more. I love that line. I've already chosen it as one of the readings for my own funeral."

Having been focused entirely on the imminence of her own death, Dawna was surprised to hear Father George speak of his. He was so big and strong. It had never occurred to her that he would die. A new thought came to her: If death is going to happen to everyone—the big and the strong, the weak and the poor, the good and the bad— maybe her own dying was not a punishment from God, as she had secretly believed. She looked into the sand picture again. Her eyes searched out the pink feathers in the sea of darks. What she needed was a new picture of herself.

"God," she heard herself say in the emptiness of her soul, "It would be so much easier to die if I thought you loved me."

Father George had no way of hearing Dawna's inner plea.

"Dawna, I want to ask you about something. Have you ever heard of the Sacrament of Anointing of the Sick?"

"Well, I've heard of it, I think, but I don't remember much about it."

"Jesus was born because God wanted to get closer to us. Did you know that Jesus spent most of his time with sick people—the ones in trouble, the ones with diseases, the blind ones, the crippled ones, and the ones possessed by spirits of self-hatred and insanity? Almost always, the first thing Jesus did was touch sick people; he put his hands on them. He prayed, and his love flowed out to them.

"In the sacraments, Jesus can touch us—again and again and again. Jesus' healing power comes to us, and we proclaim together that God is real, that God loves, that God heals, that we belong to God. In the Sacrament of Anointing of the Sick, I touch the sick person's head and trace blessed oil on the palms of her or his hands—that's called anointing. In this way, Christ himself touches that sick person.

"The fragrance of the oil always makes me think of a garden in spring. I never know exactly what kind of healing will take place. Usually I don't see medical recovery, and that's hard. Sometimes I don't see any sign of change at all. But I don't worry about that. God's best work is done in secret. God knows what each person needs, and that's what God gives.

A whole new picture started to take shape.

"Dawna, I want to celebrate the Sacrament of Anointing here, with you, in a day or two."

Dawna's breathing had become more labored. "Yes," she answered.

Father George left. Dawna remained awake awhile longer. She had asked Father George to turn the sand picture upside down before he left. The violets and the blues and the tiny feathers of pink were still falling quietly from the top. Dawna watched as a whole new picture started to take shape.

Unexpected Reunion

The next morning, Father George went immediately to Veronica Shields and told her about Dawna. The news was painful, but Veronica sensed what needed to be done. "I want to be with Dawna and you when you celebrate the sacrament, George. And I think we should ask the students who were in the Grief Support Group to come. That would mean a lot to Dawna. It will be a very powerful moment, I think. Like Tennyson wrote, 'More things are wrought by prayer than this world dreams of.'"

Father George kidded for a moment, "Do you think maybe you could get Tennyson to say a few words at my funeral?" Veronica smiled knowingly. She loved George's gentle wit, which was often at its best when he was deeply concerned about something. Time was short, though. Their first step was to find Keisha, Sarah, Simon, and Jerome.

Gathered in a Time of Crisis

Two days later, a small group gathered around Dawna's hospital bed in room 309. Sarah was there. Mike was with her. Both were shaken. Dawna's emaciated form reminded them of Sarah's grandmother's final days. But Sarah smiled as she

held out her hand to show Dawna her engagement ring. "Remember my grandma's gold ring with the roses on it? When Mike puts it on my finger on our wedding day, she'll be so happy."

Sarah wanted Dawna to share in her happiness. Sarah recalled the memorial service the group had held for Dawna's baby. Sarah remembered the ache of seeing that thin stream of smoke rising up from Mary Rose's tiny candle as it burned out. And Sarah remembered her grandmother's funeral, but the pain had changed. It wasn't nearly as sharp anymore. And the unanswered why's about suffering and death somehow seemed more bearable now. Becoming a peer counselor at Saint Monica's had helped; Sarah's grief had found solace in her reaching out to console others.

Keisha was standing next to Sarah. Jerome was not with her. Father George had tried several times to reach Jerome at his new school. Jerome received the messages but returned none of them.

2
In the process of healthy grieving, the initial intensity of painful feelings gives way to gradually lessening pain. When grief is blocked, intense pain can strike later on, unexpectedly, and much more sharply. Have you ever blocked out a difficult experience, only to have it resurface later?

3

Healthy grieving requires the courageous realization that loss has occurred, that loss is painful, and that no human person can ever be replaced. Jumping into new relationships without properly grieving existing relationships is counterproductive to any healing process. What advice might you offer Jerome at this point in the grieving process?

4

One thing is certain: When grief and death strike, we will change. But the nature of the change is up to us. Do you agree with this statement? Why or why not?

Jerome had ended his relationship with Keisha at the beginning of last year's summer vacation. He told her he was making new choices. As Keisha understood it, Jerome had decided it was better not to love than to suffer the pain of loss. Jerome left Saint Monica's in an attempt to forget everything—especially Keisha and the accident.

In Jerome's final conversation with Keisha, he had told her he was glad to be moving to a public school. "I won't have to hear about this God stuff anymore. It's junk. There's no God, and death is just the end of it all. This resurrection garbage is so stupid. So-called faith is just for people who don't want to face the truth. Well, I'm not one of them. Death is all there is at the end. So I'm just going to get what I can out of life. I'm not wrecking my head with made-up stuff."

Jerome's atheism and disappearance from her life had been a trial for Keisha. It challenged her own wavering faith. After Jerome left, Keisha began to think he might be right, that maybe there really was no God, no afterlife. It became difficult for her to pray. She was afraid she'd find out that no one was listening—maybe no one ever had. Keisha stopped praying altogether. She kept going to Sunday Mass because she didn't want her parents to know she'd stopped believing. But on Sundays, in the pew, she sat without hearing, without seeing.

Thus, it was awkward for Keisha when Father George asked her to participate in the Sacrament of Anointing of the Sick for Dawna. She agreed to even though she didn't want to. She dreaded what she expected would be yet another experience of empty ritual. Now Keisha looked down at Dawna and felt doomed. Her knees were shaking as she recalled ominous images from a poem she once read:

> I am like a flag unfurled facing far horizons.
> I sense the oncoming winds through which I must
>   survive,
> while the things below me remain quiet, rest unmoving:
> doors still close gently, and in the chimneys is silence,
> windows do not tremble, and the dust lies
>   undisturbed—
>
> Then I know the storm's approach and am as turbulent
> as the sea. I flutter, strained to my limit; I reach
> and fall back, only to hurl myself outward again
> and find myself utterly alone in the great storm.
>
> (Rainer Maria Rilke)

The desolate tone of the poem haunted Keisha now. Its sense of foreboding had stayed with her, piercing her soul like a sharp thorn. As she stood at the deathbed of a girl nearly her own age, Keisha was in turmoil. Was it better to have no faith or to meet death and grief with a God she could not see?

Keisha had no answer.

She knew only that she felt alone, as if caught in a wild and sinister storm that was threatening to swallow her up in its dreaded embrace. Her feet had nothing to stand on, nothing other than the word of God she had trusted so long ago. But she could not trust again.

The questions still echoed in her soul.

Ms. Shields was calm. Standing at Dawna's bedside took her back to the night she had stood at her brother's deathbed in the emergency ward of this same hospital. Ms. Shields had grown so much since then. The questions that had tormented her at the time of David's death still echoed in her soul, but they were no longer a torment. She was sad, and she yearned for the day she would be reunited with her brother, but she no longer wondered where death had taken him.

She stroked Dawna's brow. As she did, she saw not so much a person on the brink of death as a person on the brink of life. In her confusion and grief over David, Ms. Shields had touched upon the truth. Now, as Dawna lay dying, she clung to that same truth:

> "Set your troubled hearts at rest. Trust in God always; trust also in me. There are many dwelling-places in my Father's house. . . . I am going to prepare a place for you. And if I go and prepare a place for you, I shall come again and take you to myself, so that where I am you may be also." (John 14:1–4)

Entrusted to Grace

Simon was not present. Father George was surprised. "I'll be there," Simon had said. He had sounded so certain. Father George went ahead and put on his plain purple stole. He took a small vial and a gold pyx, a special container for consecrated Hosts, from his black bag. He opened his book of prayers.

"May God's peace be with all of you," he began. "We have gathered here with Dawna in the name of our Lord, Jesus Christ, the One who restored the sick to health and raised the dead to life. This same Lord is with us now as we recall the words of the Apostle James: 'Are there any among you who are sick? Let them call for the elders of the church, and let them pray over them and anoint them in the name of the Lord. This prayer, made in faith, will save them'" (5:14–15).

"Let us entrust our dying sister, Dawna, to the grace and power of Jesus Christ, that he may ease her suffering and grant her health and salvation."

Keisha took a step back; her sense of foreboding was suddenly unbearable.

Ms. Shields opened the Bible and handed it to Sarah. Sarah remembered being amazed at her brother's clear strong voice when he read at her grandmother's funeral. She was surprised to hear the clarity and strength in her own voice as she began to read from Paul's Letter to the Romans:

> "Throughout it all, overwhelming victory is ours through him who loved us. For I am convinced that there is nothing in death or life, in the realm of spirits or super-human powers, in the world as it is or the world as it shall be, in the forces of the universe, in heights or depths—nothing in all creation that can separate us from the love of God in Christ Jesus our Lord." (8:37–39)

Sarah took Mike's hand. She remembered how Mike had held her hand during her grandmother's funeral. Mike's steadfastness had helped Sarah begin to understand that love is stronger than death. She had been amazed to discover that all her grieving and mourning had not destroyed her love of her grandmother. In fact, she loved her grandmother even more now, almost two years after her grandmother's death, than she ever had before.

Rage That Turns to Peace

A few moments after Sarah's reading, Simon entered the room. He stationed himself at the foot of the bed. His face was tearstained yet set like stone. Father George and the others were glad to see him but were alarmed by his appearance.

The day before, when Father George had told Simon about Dawna, Simon had felt a surge of anger. After their brief conversation, Simon went to the graveyard. He stormed up to Sash's grave and saw the single daisy he had placed on it a couple of days before to help take away the bareness. The daisy, a weed actually, was one he had picked in the ditch outside the cemetery. As he caught sight of the flower, now withered and ugly, his rage went out of control. He ground the defenseless thing under his heel until its petals were all torn off and blackened. He was breathing heavily, taking great gulps of air, his heart was racing, and sweat was pouring from him.

5

Many waters cannot quench
  love,
no flood can sweep it away.
          (Song of Songs 8:7)

Do you believe that the writer of the Song of Songs is correct? Why or why not?

Without warning, he exploded, shouting at his dead brother: "How could you? How could you do that to me? Why didn't you come to us? Why didn't you tell us you were going down? Why did you have to kill yourself—didn't you care about us at all? Do you have any idea of the pain you caused everybody? Sash, why? Why, why, oh, God, why?" Simon's torrent of questions rushed out like flaming arrows. He gasped and gulped for air, tears pouring down on his brother's grave. He fell to the ground, limp and sobbing.

Simon lay motionless in the cemetery. He had been holding his rage inside for such a long time. With his eyes shut tight, Simon remembered something that had been said in the Grief Support Group: Grieving is primarily grieving for the self. The statement had made no sense to Simon then, but it did now. Simon ached over what Sash had suffered, but the worst pain was what Simon himself had suffered: the loss of Sash's trust in himself and in the rest of the family, the loss of his twin—his friend, his partner, his "other self."

6

A heart filled with bitterness has no room for anything else. God designed the human body with built-in healing mechanisms. When we are sick to our stomach, we sometimes need to vomit. Similarly, when we feel sick at heart, we need to bring up painful emotion. A heart emptied of its rage, its bitterness, and its grim refusals is a heart ready to be filled with good things. What do you think might have happened to Simon if he had continued to bottle up his rage?

Simon got up slowly. He had expected to feel shame if he ever let loose his tirade against Sash, but he didn't. Instead, he felt relief. Spewing out his long-held bitter rage created a space inside Simon's heart. He was amazed to find his love of Sash flowing into this newly created space. It felt good. He did not understand what was happening to him, but he felt lighter, more alive. He felt closer to Sash now than he had since before Sash committed suicide.

Simon went home. Hope had stirred in his soul.

The next day, however, as he was getting dressed to go to Centenary Hospital, Simon's anger rose again. The thought of praying to God around Dawna's deathbed stabbed his heart, and the rage returned. This time, it was much more fierce. The magnitude of his rage scared him. He did not understand it; he had thought his anger had all been poured out on Sash's grave the day before. He had thought he'd made peace with his brother.

Simon had not known that something else lay under his rage against Sash: his rage against God. He collapsed on his bed and covered his face with his hands. A great storm erupted. His tone was violent—as violent and accusatory as he could make it. Now the flaming arrows were shooting out at God: "You call yourself a God of love? Where were you when Sash was going down? Why didn't you save him? You're supposed to be the one with all the power! Where was your power then? You deserted my brother—and you deserted me. You'll never get my heart. Never! Never!"

Suddenly, Simon pulled himself up. He would go to the hospital. At the time, he did not understand his own motivation for going. Now he was standing at the foot of Dawna's bed. Father George was blessing the fragrant oil: "Praise to you, God the Holy Spirit, the Consoler. You heal our sickness with your mighty power."

Simon slowly turned red, as though his blood had begun to boil. Inwardly, he reproached God: "Why should Dawna or anyone else praise you when you abandon people in their hour of greatest need? Praise is the last thing you'll be getting from me."

Father George continued: "Lord God, with faith in you, our sister Dawna will be anointed with this holy oil. Ease her suffering and strengthen her in her weakness. We ask this through Christ our Lord. Amen." Father George then put oil on his thumb and began tracing the sign of the cross on Dawna's forehead. As he did, he prayed: "Through this holy anointing may the Lord in his love and mercy help you with the grace of the Holy Spirit. May the Lord who frees you from sin save you and raise you up."

Then he took Dawna's hands and gently traced a cross of oil on each. Simon struggled to control his rising rage. Seeing Dawna's pale hands reminded him of how Sash had looked in his coffin—his skin waxen and unnatural. Simon's hatred of God peaked. He watched Father George conclude what seemed a pitifully futile ritual with Dawna's hands.

But then Simon looked into Dawna's face and did not see futility. It seemed impossible, but her eyes looked as if they were filled with light. In spite of himself, he couldn't help remembering the feel of Sash's love rushing into his soul in the graveyard.

Ms. Shields was reading aloud. It was a prayer she had written for Dawna:

> You who are God,
> you of unimaginable compassion
> and tenderness,
> draw us into yourself.
> You, Unseen,
> whom we love,
> you whom we desire,
> pull us closer.
> Caress us
> with the sweet assurance
> of our utter safety in you—
> you who lay your own self bare
> and without defense before us,
> you who subject yourself
> to our ridicule
> and rejection of you.
> Dearest God,
> you open yourself to us,
> yearning to pour your own great fires
> into our oh-so-tiny hearts—
> those strange, wild little kingdoms you ache to enter,
> even now.

The huddle of people around Dawna's bed were startled by Ms. Shields's prayer. They were jolted awake by it, as if from a heavy sleep. Dawna had never thought of her own heart as any kind of kingdom, much less thought of God aching to enter such a place. It had not occurred to Simon that God had opened himself to ridicule. Simon's rejection of God had been savage and merciless. And something quickened in Keisha when Ms. Shields spoke of yearning. Could it be that she, Keisha, yearned to be pulled into the embrace of an unseen Lover? For one fleeting moment, she felt both terror and awe.

They were jolted awake by the prayer.

Father George read aloud:

Let dawn bring news of your faithful love,
for I place my trust in you;
show me the road I must travel
for you to relieve my heart.

(Psalm 143:8)

All at once, Keisha knew she could no longer face the great storm alone. Yet she had no faith. What road could she possibly travel that would relieve her heart?

Dawna's eyes fell, in turn, on each of those gathered around her bed. "All of you," she breathed, "you're like my family. I never really had any family until you."

In that instant, Simon's rage was gone. Dawna's tenderness had reached down to the very root of his being. He felt so close to her. He felt needed. His heart melted like ice in summer. Since his arrival in room 309, Simon had struggled not to give voice to the anger that had erupted twice already, once in the cemetery and once in his bedroom. The last thing he wanted was to get emotional in front of everybody. However, for this brief moment, he wished with all his heart that he could give voice to his love.

But Simon could speak not a single word. Clumsily, he reached out and caressed Dawna's foot through her white blanket.

Father George prayed the concluding words of the sacrament, then invited all present to recite the Lord's Prayer. Of their own accord, they joined hands and prayed aloud together. Father George gave Dawna a Host taken from the small gold pyx. She took the Host and, with water to help her swallow, she consumed it.

Father George offered Communion to the entire group, and each person in turn accepted a Host. Then he gave the final blessing: "May he raise you up on eagles' wings, bear you on the breath of dawn, make you to shine like the sun, and hold you in the palm of his hand. And may God bless us all in the name of the Father and of the Son and of the Holy Spirit. Amen."

As the sacramental rite concluded, six individuals found themselves drawn together in God's tender embrace of a dying friend. It was difficult for them to think of leaving. What helped them to go, finally, was the doctor's opinion that Dawna had at least several days still to live. This need not be their final good-bye. One by one, they left.

Keisha was the last to go. She hesitated a moment, then bent down and kissed Dawna on the forehead. Dawna had not been kissed like this before. With Keisha's kiss, a flood-

He felt so close to her. He felt needed.

gate opened inside Dawna's soul. Unsure of how to deal with her own surge of tenderness, Keisha left quickly, too quickly to see the change in Dawna. As Keisha was running down the hall, Dawna was crying tears of joy, the tears shed by one who feels loved.

My Beloved, Come Away

A Fearless Departure

That evening, Dawna died.

Father George and Ms. Shields, Sarah, Mike, Keisha, and Simon would be shocked when they heard the news. They had left believing they'd see Dawna again. But death—like birth—comes at a time of its own choosing, frequently when least expected.

In Dawna's dying hours, she had experienced peace for the first time in her life. In the Sacrament of Anointing of the Sick, Dawna had been surrounded by people who cared about her, by people who were openly proclaiming a God of love. In that moment, Dawna's guilt left her, and the name Mary Rose drifted painlessly, peacefully through her consciousness. In the same moment, Dawna no longer feared facing God. By the time of Keisha's kiss, Dawna was serene, relaxed in body, mind, and soul. Tranquil at last, Dawna moved into her dying.

No one could be seen standing at Dawna's bedside when death came. But Dawna did not die alone.

My beloved speaks and says to me:
"Arise, my love, my fair one,
   and come away;
for now the winter is past,
   the rain is over and gone.
The flowers appear on the earth;
   the time of singing has come,
and the voice of the turtledove
   is heard in our land.
The fig tree puts forth its figs,
   and the vines are in blossom;
   they give forth fragrance.
Arise, my love, my fair one,
   and come away."

(Song of Songs 2:10–13)

Broken Open

The news of Dawna's death hit Simon and Keisha the hardest. Both were battling with a God they needed desperately but dared not trust. For both, Dawna's sudden death was like salt rubbed into a wound.

His soul in flames, Simon exploded in yet another raving frenzy against God. He stood outside the graveyard gates, near the ditch where the daisies grew. "The God who fails! You are the God who fails! You failed Sash, you failed me, and now you've failed Dawna. I tried—I really tried to trust you again, and you betrayed me. You are a God who does nothing—at the critical moment, you do *nothing*. She called us family. We were all she had, and you took us away when she needed us most. We prayed for her healing, and you gave her death. I *hate* you, God. *Hate* you!"

Simon threw himself into the ditch and buried his head and his hoarse cries in the tall grass. Occasionally he reached out and punched lamely at the ground. Then he sank into silence. He wondered if Sash's final moments had been like this. With a kind of horror, Simon realized he was heading down the same road Sash had followed to his death: the road of despair. Simon remained in the ditch, paralyzed by fear.

At that moment, Simon knew that the power over his life was his own. He was free to live and equally free to die.

Sash, in his suicide note, had asked Simon to join him in death. A year earlier, in the Grief Support Group, Simon had known he could not do as Sash had asked. But now, today in this ditch, the urge to commit suicide was not coming from Sash's note. The urge to die was coming directly from the depths of Simon's own tormented soul.

Simon's heart was pounding when a different voice rose up from inside of him—a voice unfamiliar, yet strangely his own: "God, I am in hell. Failure is all I can see; pain is all I can feel. Walls so high I can't climb them, can't even see over them. There's no help. No door. No hope. No way out. I scream inside myself, and my voice is heard nowhere. Endless, endless pain. I am finally beaten. I am being sucked into this graveyard. . . . God, help me!"

With that cry for help, Simon's heart was broken. Broken open.

> The power over his life was his own.

A Woman of Courage

Sarah and Mike got the news of Dawna's death from Ms. Shields. Mike put his arm around Sarah, but Sarah had already found her own strength: "It's okay. Dawna is okay," she said. Sarah put her arm around Mike's waist, and the two

7
Without knowing it, Sarah was talking about the communion of saints, the union in Christ of those on earth and those in heaven. What have you learned in other courses about the communion of saints? How would you explain it more fully to Sarah?

8
Have you ever experienced a sort of healing in which nothing changed outwardly, but on the inside, emotionally, you felt very much changed?

continued down the hall. "I never thought of it before, but now Dawna can be with Mary Rose. Maybe that's why she died sooner than anybody thought she would."

Sarah could picture Dawna's happiness. At the same time, she pictured her grandmother. In her heart, Sarah looked forward to the day she'd be reunited with her grandmother in heaven. But Sarah was quite happy not to die yet. She loved Mike, and Mike loved her. Like her grandmother, she had a life to live on earth. Sarah had learned that this life is good and that in the next life, there is even more goodness to come.

A short while later, Ms. Shields found Keisha and asked her to come to her office. When Keisha heard the news, her face went dark. She crumpled into tears. "Oh, God," Keisha wailed, "I thought the Sacrament of Anointing of the Sick was supposed to help people. It seems like it made Dawna's death come even faster. Why is God so hard to understand? It's like even if we try to follow God, we still get burned. I just don't understand anything anymore. What's the point in trusting God? We're just going to die anyway. Jerome was right. Jerome was right."

Ms. Shields knew that Keisha had not fully understood the sacrament. Keisha had not considered the possibility that Dawna's healing might have made her more open to death, ready to accept the inevitable, ready to move into the newness and promise of the next life, ready at last to fall into the arms of God.

In her own crises of faith, Ms. Shields had learned that God's ways of healing are not our ways. She herself had so often wished that God would cure her brother of his manic-depressive illness. God hadn't. Her will to trust God, to hold on to her faith, to be a more compassionate person, to love her brother even through grief—these had been the only signs of hope to which she could cling. As for the rest, Ms. Shields finally had to trust that the mystery of God was a mystery of love. She knew now that the kind of healing God brings is often invisible to the eyes, felt in the heart alone.

Ms. Shields could have tried to explain all that to the weeping Keisha, but she didn't.

Instead, Ms. Shields gave her young student a big challenge. "Keisha, God is the one you need now, the only one who can answer your heart. You are a woman of courage. Go and search for God; you will discover a God who has been searching for you."

In her young life, Keisha had not often heard herself referred to as a woman, much less as a woman of courage. Still, despite the compelling image of herself as an adult, Keisha could not rise.

"But I don't know how to pray. I don't know how."

"Then maybe just say, 'My heart is ready.' God can take it from there."

Mingled Tears

The Choice to Move Forward

Simon could hear the wind rustling the tall grass in the ditch where he was lying. He wasn't sure, but he thought he had slept for a while. He was so tired. He struggled to sit up. The ditch was filled with white daisies, many more than he had realized. He saw so many, in fact, that the side of the road seemed alive with white-and-yellow blooms bobbing in the wind. He had a sudden urge to pick every one of them, to gather them up into one huge bunch. Excitedly, he reached over to pull the first one out of the ground.

Then he stopped. "No," he thought. "I'll leave them. Better that they bloom here by the side of the road where they were planted." And so began Simon's determination to live whatever came his way—the hurts, the losses, and even the rages. He made the decision that day to move forward into the mystery and challenges of his own life. It was a choice he would have to make again and again and again.

Simon pulled himself to his feet. "One foot in front of the other," he said to himself, "I'll just keep putting one foot in front of the other." Simon walked down the road and past the black graveyard gate. As he looked up, all along the road that stretched in front of him, there were daisies as far as he could see.

Love Never Ceases

Father George went back to Centenary Hospital to pick up the few personal belongings from Dawna's room. Among them was the sand picture. Sitting in his car, Father George turned the picture upside down; he never could resist the urge to do this. But then he did something he had not done before. He shook it hard, as hard as he could.

Instantly, rich dark blues filled the frame. The rose-pink feathers broke into a million tiny pieces and freely dispersed themselves throughout the expanse of darks. Father George saw a night sky come alive with an explosion of bright stars. It reminded him of a passage he had read last Christmas, by a writer named Frederick Buechner, about the coming of Jesus to the world:

9

On the night before Easter, Catholic churches turn off all their lights. As the people stand together in the darkness, a single candle is lit and an unaccompanied voice sings the Easter Proclamation, or *Exsultet,* which contains the words

> Rejoice, O earth, in shining
> splendor,
> radiant in the brightness of
> your King!
> Christ has conquered! Glory
> fills you!
> Darkness vanishes for ever!

Recall Simon in the graveyard. He rose up from his own darkness. What did he conquer when he decided to move forward? What glory do you think might have filled him that day? Why must Simon make the choice to move forward "again and again and again"? What might he need to do to keep moving toward the day when, for him, darkness vanishes forever?

The darkness was shattered like glass, and the glory flooded through with the light of a thousand suns. A new star blazed forth where there had never been a star before, and the air was filled with the bright wings of angels, the night sky came alive with the glittering armies of God, and a great hymn of victory rose up from them—Glory to God in the highest. . . . This is how, after all the weary centuries of waiting, the light is said finally to have come into the world.

In his forty-three years, Father George had looked into the face of death many times. It never got easy. It never stopped hurting. It always shocked and saddened him. However, his experience with death had brought him more than trauma and pain. As he drove away from the hospital, Father George thought about his own funeral and about the explosion of lights in Dawna's picture frame. He remembered the poetry of Tennyson, who said of human beings, "They are but broken lights of thee."

Father George was thinking that at the time of his own death, those he loved would be filled with their own shock, sadness, and pain. As he drove, catching yellow light after yellow light, Father George decided on one more passage he wanted read at his funeral:

> But this I call to mind,
>   and therefore I have hope:
>
> The steadfast love of the LORD never ceases,
>   his mercies never come to an end;
> they are new every morning;
>   great is your faithfulness.
> . . . .
> The LORD is good to those who wait for him,
>   to the soul that seeks him.
>
> (Lamentations 3:21–25)

In the Still and Quiet Night

Keisha went home after her talk with Ms. Shields. Her black cat, no longer the tiny kitten of the previous year, was in her arms. She rocked it like a baby. In moments, the cat slipped into a contented, purring sleep.

Keisha felt crushed by the weight of Dawna's death. Since hearing the news that afternoon, she had found the hours long and without peace. In fact, for Keisha, life itself had become long and without peace. Gently, she stroked the cat's soft, sleek fur. The cat, actually, was quite an ordinary one, but at this moment, its fur felt silken rich. She could find no other comfort. Tonight Keisha's mind was far too weary to think any thoughts at all. And her head, still spinning from the torture of unanswered questions, ached from having cried too much. But in her soul, something stirred. Taking a deep, deliberate breath, she whispered a single statement into the silky softness nestled in her lap: "My heart is not ready, God, but come in anyway."

Several years were to pass before Keisha could understand what had happened in her that night. At the age of twenty-one, she would write a poem about what occurred the night she allowed God in:

Within the still and quiet night we met.
Earlier, there had been thunder
and pounding driving torrents
heavy black drops searing where they fell.
Now the misty air was silent soft.
Ah the beauty of your tender word,
as smooth rose petals touching burning skin
their fragrance nestling round me as I stood,
my rigid body yielding, yielding, yielding.
I heard you speak.
I heard your voice.
With quivering lips, with unclenched hand I stood,
my being poised, expectant, bent on you.
At last my feet could stay a moment, calm,
pausing in their restless nervous flight.
Intent upon your voice I did not know
that you had stilled the tense uneasy motion
and all that moved within me was my breath,
your breath.
I breathed you in and held you in myself
and in myself you held me. So I lived,
not I but you, and yet I lived.
I lived to be in you,
as all my cries of pain, of fear, of loneliness,
the dark and loathsome burdens I had made
you took from me,
you took in gentleness and joy,
you emptied me that I might overflow.
Your arms around me bore me up,
my tears and yours were mingled as they fell,
within the still and quiet night.

Appendices

Appendix A

Hospice: Compassionate Care for the Dying

Two Main Choices

Patients who are suffering from terminal illnesses (illnesses that will result in death, regardless of medical treatment) often desire three things: to die with dignity, to die with as little pain as possible, and to die with the awareness of the loving attention of family and friends.

A particular type of health care promotes this way of dying for terminal patients. It is called hospice.

What Is Hospice?

The term *hospice* originated in the Middle Ages. Hospices were shelters provided for travelers, especially travelers who were poor. Hospices were often maintained by members of religious orders who took seriously the Gospel call to shelter the homeless and feed the hungry.

Today, the word *hospice* has a broader meaning. Hospice care is a community-based response to the needs of terminally ill persons and their families. Hospice focuses on the quality of life of the dying person, rather than on attempting to increase the length of time the person has to live. Hospice care is dedicated to helping terminally ill people spend their final days, weeks, or months at home (or in a homelike environment within a hospital or nursing home), alert and with minimal pain, among people they cherish. In contemporary terms, hospice provides a place to rest on the "journey" to death and beyond.

A thirty-seven-year-old terminally ill patient summed up the goal of hospice in this way: "[Hospice] cannot add days to your life but [it] can absolutely add life to your days."

The first modern hospice was founded in London in 1968. Cicely Saunders, the founder, believed that existing health care institutions ignored the special needs of the dying. The hospice she founded was based on this conviction: "You matter to the last moment of your life, and we will do all we can, not only to help you die peacefully, but to live until you die."

The hospice movement did not begin as an offshoot of any particular religion. But hospice care is a beautiful reflection of the attitude Saint Paul said is required of a Christian: "You are to be clothed in heartfelt compassion" (Colossians 3:12).

The first hospice in the United States began in New Haven, Connecticut, in 1974. Now more than twenty-one hundred hospices care for people in every state of the union. Nearly three hundred thousand people a year choose hospice as their way to approach death. And more and more people are becoming aware of the hospice option. A recent Gallup poll found that 86 percent of those surveyed would choose to be cared for and die at home if they learned they were terminally ill.

How Does Hospice Work?

Hospices neither speed up nor slow down the process of dying. Rather, they focus on the quality of life—whatever the number of a person's remaining days. The dying patient's home is the usual setting for hospice care, but such care may be found in hospitals, nursing homes, and independent facilities as well. In every case, a homelike environment is the goal.

Joan Leslie Taylor, who worked for several years as a hospice volunteer, provides a description of the goals and methods of hospice care:

- The goal of treatment is comfort rather than cure.
- Pain control is a priority. Medications are used, but other treatments, such as massage, visualizations, music, heat, activities, and visitors are used as well.
- All symptoms are treated to enhance the patient's comfort. Attention is paid to diet, skin care, bowel and bladder function, nausea, and edema.
- Care encompasses the physical, the emotional, the mental, and the spiritual.
- An interdisciplinary team approach is used. The team is directed by a physician, either the medical director of the hospice program or the patient's own personal physician, and includes, social workers, registered nurses, attendants, clergy and trained volunteers.
- The unit of care is the whole family, which includes friends caring for the patient as well. The hospice team provides emotional and practical support to the family and the patient.
(*In the Light of Dying,* page xiii)

A Hospice Story

Many stories have been told about the positive effect of hospice on the lives of dying persons and their families. Joyce Heil is a hospice nurse who found that one of her most moving hospice experiences involved members of her own family:

As a registered nurse working in the hospice area, I have had the privilege of walking the last miles of life with many patients and their families. Providing symptom management, education, and support during the final months of patients' lives gives them, in many instances, the ability to stay in their own home. At home they can be surrounded by the people they love in an environment in which they are comfortable.

Though I have been involved in many deaths over the past year, the one that has affected me the most happened a few years ago in my own family. My sister's father-in-law, Norm, was diagnosed with terminal cancer of the lung. Having been divorced many years earlier, Norm lived in a boarding house with an old friend. Gradually it became evident that he could no longer care for himself, so my sister, Jean, and her husband, Bill, decided to take Norm into their home for the last months of his life. This had been a hard family decision. Jean and Bill talked to their children about what this decision would mean in their lives. At the time, Amanda was eight years old and Collin was twelve. Collin gave up his room so that a hospital bed could be set up. A hospice nurse came to the house to teach the family how to care for Grandpa Norm.

Though Jean and Bill took time off from work as much as possible, there were many hours when Collin was called upon to be the primary caregiver for Grandpa Norm. Collin admitted that he was afraid Grandpa Norm would die when he was there alone with him. Jean and Bill knew that they were expecting a lot from a twelve-year-old, and the hospice nurse talked to Collin about this and his feelings many times. But Collin became Norm's primary caregiver even when everyone was at home. He knew best what Grandpa Norm needed and how he wanted things done.

I remember stopping at my sister's home during this time and finding Collin sitting with Grandpa Norm. When Norm wanted to be moved, I volunteered to help, and it was Collin who told me, a registered nurse, how to do it the way "Grandpa likes it." He moved him and gave him a bedpan, and some water to drink. Collin did all this with a tenderness that brought tears to my eyes.

Registered nurses and nursing assistants came to the home for a few hours daily. They provided the physical and emotional support the family needed. This support and guidance allowed Jean, Bill, Amanda, and Collin to be with Grandpa Norm until his death late one afternoon when my sister was alone with him. Collin had been with him all day, and when Jean came home from work, she spent some time with Norm. The phone rang, and when Jean got back from answering the phone, he had died. They were all thankful that the hospice program had allowed Grandpa Norm to die at home, surrounded by the people he loved and who loved him.

Dying Is an Act of Community

The benefits of hospice care to the dying patient are obvious. Less obvious but equally important are the benefits to the community in general. Cicely Saunders explained: "The dying need the community, its help, fellowship, care and attention, which will quieten their distress and fears and enable them to go peacefully. The community needs the dying to make it think of eternal issues and to make it listen and give to others." Hospice care calls forth the healing gifts in all of us: compassion, support, comfort, companionship, listening.

Those who care lovingly for the dying are deepened in their own compassion, enriched in their insights about life and death, and challenged to face life's greatest and most mysterious realities.

Appendix B

Euthanasia: Mercy or Murder?

Some Hypothetical Questions

A seventeen-year-old, depressed after breaking up with his girlfriend, flunks his driver's test for the third time. He tells a friend, "I wish I were dead." Should we kill him to put him out of his pain? A ninety-two-year-old woman is dying. She has been suffering from terminal inoperable cancer, has no living relatives, and has been peacefully preparing for death. She suffers a massive stroke. Should we follow the "do not resuscitate" order and allow her to die?

Most would easily agree that the depressed seventeen-year-old should live and that the ninety-two-year-old woman should be allowed to die. However, many other situations arise for which there are no easy or obvious answers. Often we disagree on what to do and why.

Should a physician have the legal right to give a fatal injection to a chronically ill patient if that patient has requested such an injection? Should the father of a fourteen-year-old girl with cerebral palsy be allowed to kill her in order to save her from what he sees as a life of suffering? What about a young mother left quadriplegic and nearly brain-dead from a car accident: at a public cost of several thousand dollars a day for her hospital care, what treatment should be given and for how long?

Questions like these are getting tougher and tougher in recent years. Why? First, new technologies are giving humanity possibilities and choices never before available. New choices lead to new consequences, requiring new and harder questions. Second, our society is drawing less and less from a common set of values and principles by which to live. More diverse points of view increase the challenge of finding common ground for discussion and action. And finally, we are focusing more on the short-term "rights" of individuals than on the long-term good of humanity. In other words, we are often failing to consider the long-term effects of our actions on society.

Our answers to such tough questions are important because they can affect lives and deaths every day. They also reveal to us our operative beliefs about the meaning of life, the function of suffering, the identity of God, and the value we place on community.

What Is Euthanasia?

Euthanasia is one of the most difficult and controversial medical issues of our time. Euthanasia (sometimes called mercy killing) refers to an action or omission that *intentionally* causes death, thus bringing an end to a person's suffering. Injecting a patient with a lethal dosage of painkilling medication, with the intent to cause death rather than to manage pain, is an example of euthanasia.

Euthanasia must not be confused with the decision of a dying person or his or her relatives to stop extraordinary medical care to prolong life. In cases where death is imminent, it is possible to cease extraordinary actions (such as dialysis or artificial respiration) that prolong life, and instead control the pain of the patient and allow him or her to die in peace and comfort. Such a choice is not an act of euthanasia; it is, in fact, a hallmark of hospice care (see appendix A).

Euthanasia in Practice

Euthanasia is illegal in the United States, but support for legalization is growing. Many supporters look to the example of the Netherlands, where laws concerning euthanasia are relaxed enough that it can be practiced under certain circumstances. Daniel Callahan, a leader in the field of medical ethics, describes the conditions that must be met to allow euthanasia in the Netherlands:

> First, the person requesting euthanasia must be a competent adult, and his or her request one that has been persistently made over time. Second, the patient must be in a state of "unbearable" pain or suffering. Third, the independent judgment of a second doctor must be obtained to verify the first two conditions. In addition to these requirements, existing laws require that there be accurate reporting by the physician of the cause of death. (*The Troubled Dream of Life,* pages 112–113)

According to Callahan, the experience of the Netherlands has not been positive. It is estimated, for example, that three or four thousand cases of euthanasia take place each year. But in only about three hundred cases do physicians fulfill the requirement that the cause of death be reported. It is therefore impossible to determine whether the conditions for legal euthanasia are being met.

Dr. Karel Gunning, a Dutch physician who opposes euthanasia, told a meeting of the Canadian Senate:

> "Instead of killing the pain, they're killing the patient. The most important message I would like to give you is that once you start considering killing as a solution for one problem then you quickly might have a thousand problems for which killing is a solution."

Gunning believes that the system in the Netherlands is open to a great deal of abuse. He told of a psychiatrist who helped a chronically depressed woman kill herself. The woman was otherwise healthy. Other doctors gave lethal doses of drugs to patients who were not considered to be dying. But because they could prove that the patients wanted to die prematurely, the doctors and the psychiatrist could not be prosecuted for wrongdoing ("Euthanasia Opens Door to Misuse, MD Says").

The original intent of legalizing euthanasia in the Netherlands was to give patients more control over their choices regarding death. The actual result has been an immense increase in doctors' control over patients' dying. Laws can be made, but it is difficult to prevent their abuse. Daniel Callahan sums up the situation:

> In short, the evidence suggests that, at best, the present practice in the Netherlands has laid the groundwork for a severely slippery slope. At worst—which I am convinced is already the case—the slide down that slope has begun. (*The Troubled Dream of Life,* page 114)

The Risks of the Slippery Slope

The slippery slope Callahan speaks of is filled with risks. When something that has been unthinkable becomes thinkable, it is possible that it will then become justifiable, praiseworthy, and, eventually, mandatory. Those who accept the option of euthanasia must contend with a multitude of related issues and questions. If euthanasia is acceptable, *when* is it acceptable? Should all citizens over the age of sixty-five be subject to euthanasia in order to save taxpayers the cost of taking care of an older population? Should terminally ill patients be made to die prematurely so that their healthy organs can be used for transplants? Should a severely ill patient be denied treatment so that her or his family can avoid high medical costs? Saying yes or no to euthanasia is not a simple task.

The slippery slope leads to other risks as well:
- Doctors may become sanctioned killers rather than healers, leading to a breakdown of trust between doctors and patients.
- The primary goal of health care may become unclear.
- Dying may become a "duty," especially in cases where high costs are involved; patients are likely to feel unwanted and unloved.
- Those who are old or ill may begin to live in fear.

The Voice of the Church

The Catholic church, having considered the risks of euthanasia and the nature of human life, teaches clearly that "*euthanasia is a grave violation of the law of God*, since it is the deliberate and morally unacceptable killing of a human person" (*The Gospel of Life*, number 65).

The Dignity of Life

All the church's teachings on human life are grounded in the firm belief that all human beings are created in the image of God. The Book of Genesis tells us:

> Then God said, "Let us make humankind in our
>   image, according to our likeness. . . ."
> So God created humankind in his image,
>   in the image of God he created them;
>   male and female he created them.
>
> (1:26–27)

As creatures made in God's image, people have immense God-given dignity. Human dignity is a permanent, sacred value; it can be assaulted and violated, but it cannot be taken away. Every human being has a right to have this value respected fully. Actions such as murder, abortion, and euthanasia attack the dignity of human life.

The Meaning of Suffering

In light of human dignity, what is the meaning of suffering? Our first impulse in the face of suffering is likely to be to run from it, to get as far from it as possible. But pain and suffering are an unavoidable part of life. Try as we might to avoid suffering, we will experience it at one time or another. Denying that fact can lead to destructive behavior and a sense that life is meaningless.

In the Christian understanding, lack of suffering is not necessarily a good thing. Pain, whether physical or emotional, need not make life meaningless or futile. Pain may be the passageway to real living.

Consider two examples. One is a young person who runs from every possibility of pain. He hides behind alcohol, other drugs, and promiscuous sex. He does not allow himself to dream, because he is certain that he will fail to fulfill his dreams, and failure will cause him to suffer. He quickly discards new relationships before they can

become difficult or painful. For all its busyness, his life is empty.

On the other end of the spectrum, consider a person who works hard to achieve her dreams. She makes mistakes, learns from them, and keeps going. She enters relationships with a sense of commitment, knowing she is vulnerable and capable of hurting and being hurt. Her successes and failures bring her joy and sorrow. Through both, she learns more about who she is and who she wants to become, how to love, how to become truly alive, and how to discover the richness of life.

The second person is more aware of her suffering than the first, but she is the more likely of the two to find real happiness.

Christians are called not to evade or eradicate suffering, but to enter into suffering as Jesus did, with love and hope. Even Jesus could not avoid suffering, but through his suffering came new life. For Christians, suffering is seen as sharing in the death and Resurrection of Christ. Human suffering, whether it occurs throughout life or at life's end, offers the possibility of transformation.

The Nature of Compassion

Many people argue that euthanasia is an act of compassion because it brings a person's suffering to an end. Catholic teaching exposes the flaw in this argument by pointing to the true nature of compassion.

The literal meaning of the word *compassion* is "to suffer with." Compassion requires that we be *present* with a person who is suffering, even in the most difficult and painful stages of an illness. As Pope John Paul II states, "True 'compassion' leads to sharing another's pain; it does not kill the person whose suffering we cannot bear" (*The Gospel of Life*, number 66). True compassion transforms both those who are ill and those who suffer with them.

This does not mean that painkilling medications must be avoided. Catholic teaching holds that pain should be responsibly managed. Persons in pain need not bear their suffering "heroically." The ideal, however, is for the dying patient to remain as conscious as possible because, as Pope John Paul asserts, "As they approach death people ought to be able to satisfy their moral and family duties, and above all they ought to be able to prepare in a fully conscious way for their definitive meeting with God" (*The Gospel of Life,* number 65).

A Cry for Love

If we really listen to the plea of those who are suffering and dying, we will hear not so much a plea for euthanasia but a cry for love. Human anguish calls not for hastened death but for more compassion.

Society today wants to be in control of its own destiny. It fears pain and refuses to acknowledge its own limits. Many speak of "death with dignity" as the goal of euthanasia. But dignity is not rooted in control, escape, self-interest, or manipulation. If we see our life as an article of personal property subject to our control and manipulation, we are not likely to experience joy. Instead, we may find ourselves consumed by self-interest; we run the risk of hurting ourselves and those who are weaker than we are.

Love, not control or self-interest, is the source of dignity. And in love, we are drawn to the suffering of those we love. As long as there is love, there is dignity, for the dying *and* the living, in suffering *and* in joy.

Appendix C

Capital Punishment

How did you react the last time a friend rejected or hurt you?

Did you feel the desire to "get your friend back"?

That desire is the human lust for revenge. It rises up in all of us at one time or another. Something else we all have is freedom. When harmed by another, we can freely choose our reaction. We can love or hate; we can build up or tear down.

Humanity is violated daily by humanity. And each day society must respond to this violation. As a society, how should we deal with people who violate humanity by committing violent crimes? Traditionally, there have been two answers to this question: take revenge on such offenders, or rehabilitate them.

A Brief Overview

Since ancient times, across numerous cultures, death has been the ultimate penalty for transgressors. This response to transgression is known as capital punishment, or the death penalty.

The death penalty has been legal throughout the history of the United States—although between 1967 and 1977, while the U.S. Supreme Court evaluated whether the death penalty was constitutional, no executions took place. Each state determines for itself, however, whether capital punishment will be legal in its boundaries. Methods for carrying out the death penalty have included hanging, firing squad, electrocution, lethal gas, and lethal injection. In early U.S. history, executions often took place in public, with hundreds of spectators. Today, executions usually occur late at night, with only a small group of witnesses in attendance.

Problems with the Death Penalty

A number of problems arise when we examine the use of the death penalty. The U.S. Constitution guarantees that criminal offenders are not to have "cruel and unusual" punishments inflicted upon them. Methods of execution have been modified over the years in an attempt to make death occur quickly and painlessly. But no method has been foolproof. Even the most sophisticated methods have failed due to human or technical error, causing increased suffering and violating the constitutional right of the person being executed.

Another problem arises from the potential for error in the criminal justice system. A person who has been wrongly convicted of a crime and executed cannot be brought back to life. The death sentence, once carried out, is irrevocable.

Studies have shown that the death penalty is more likely to be prescribed in cases where a murder victim is white; killers of African American victims are seldom sentenced to death. Women, too, are unlikely to receive the death sentence, even though 40 percent of U.S. homicides are committed by women. Defendants who are poor are usually unable to obtain the legal advice needed to defend themselves effectively and are more likely to receive a death sentence for a capital crime. Inconsistencies in the way the death penalty is applied among the U.S. population constitute a serious argument against its use. Some say that the death sentence is so severe that to use it at all requires absolute fairness, and absolute fairness is impossible to achieve.

Those who favor the death penalty often argue that the threat of death as a punishment prevents or deters people from committing crimes. Studies have failed to support this claim, however. States that use capital punishment tend to have higher murder rates than states that use it infrequently or not at all. Other proponents of the death penalty argue that a person who takes a life should simply lose his or hers in retribution. This is the revenge argument: The guilty party should "get what he or she deserves." This form of revenge fails to provide the criminal with an opportunity for rehabilitation—an opportunity that can transform lives and communities.

The Voice of the Church

In 1980, the Catholic bishops of the United States declared their adamant opposition to the death penalty: "We believe that in the conditions of contemporary American society, the legitimate purposes of punishment do not justify the imposition of the death penalty" (*U.S. Bishops' Statement on Capital Punishment,* page 5).

In their statement, the bishops stated the three legitimate, or lawful, purposes of punishment: retribution, deterrence, and reform. Revenge is not considered to be a legitimate purpose of punishment. According to the bishops, neither retribution, deterrence, nor reform justifies the death sentence. They explained that retribution does not require or justify a sentence of death because punishment can take far less severe forms and still be effective. The bishops also explained that the evidence does not support the claim that the threat of capital punishment deters people from committing crime. And killing a person, the bishops said, eliminates any chance he or she might have for personal reform. With death comes the end of a person's chances to change, to grow morally, and to make creative compensation for the evil he or she has brought into the world. On the basis of the stated purposes of punishment, the bishops concluded that there is no valid justification for the death penalty.

Pope John Paul II teaches that the only possible way to justify an execution would be to prove that without it public safety would be compromised. In today's prison systems, however, the pope believes, the chance of such a case would be "practically nonexistent" (*The Gospel of Life,* number 56).

Human Dignity

At the heart of Catholic teaching against the death penalty is a firm belief in the "unique worth and dignity of each person from the moment of conception, a creature made in the image and likeness of God" (*U.S. Bishops' Statement on Capital Punishment,* page 7). The U.S. bishops explained that the belief in human dignity extends even to those who have violated others:

> It is particularly important in the context of our times that this belief be affirmed with regard to those who have failed or whose lives have been distorted by suffering or hatred, even in the case of those who by their actions have failed to respect the dignity and rights of others. It is the recognition of the dignity of all human beings that has impelled the Church to minister to the needs of the outcast and the rejected and that should make us unwilling to treat the lives of even those who have taken human life as expendable. (Page 7)

No person is without her or his God-given dignity. Pope John Paul II states quite clearly, *"Not even a murderer loses his personal dignity,* and God himself pledges to guarantee this" (*The Gospel of Life,* number 9).

Jesus' Law of Love

Catholic teaching on the death penalty is rooted in Jesus' law of love:

> "You have heard that it was said, 'You shall love your neighbor and hate your enemy.' But I say to you, Love your enemies and pray for those

who persecute you, so that you may be children of your Father in heaven." (Matthew 5:43–45)

Jesus also forbids us to take revenge upon someone who has wronged us:

"You have heard that it was said, 'An eye for an eye and a tooth for a tooth.' But I say to you, Do not resist an evildoer. But if anyone strikes you on the right cheek, turn the other also; and if anyone wants to sue you and take your coat, give your cloak as well." (Matthew 5:38–40)

Another aspect of Jesus' law of love is forgiveness. After teaching his disciples the Lord's Prayer, Jesus explained further about the requirement to forgive those who have harmed us:

"If you forgive others their trespasses, your heavenly Father will also forgive you; but if you do not forgive others, neither will your Father forgive your trespasses." (Matthew 6:14–15)

Jesus himself fulfilled the requirement to forgive. While dying on the cross, suffering an unjust execution, he asked God to forgive his persecutors: "'Father, forgive them; for they do not know what they are doing'" (Luke 23:34). A short while later, he died.

The love Jesus taught about and embodied actually exists in our world. It is often found in those who are most broken and destroyed. For example, it can be seen in a group called Murder Victims' Families for Reconciliation (MVFR). In spite of their loss and grief, these relatives of murder victims uphold the law of love. They work actively to abolish the death penalty, which they consider a barbaric response to violent crime, a response that only continues the cycle of violence. In the midst of their grief, MVFR members conquer the human impulse for revenge. In doing so, they endorse and illuminate the urgency to forgive. They choose not to meet violence with more violence because such action does not bring healing. Love brings healing.

The hallmark of Christian faithfulness is this: Love and forgive, love and forgive, love and forgive. In this action, evil itself is transformed. No limit must ever be placed on either love or forgiveness. No matter how hard it gets, we need to keep on loving and keep on forgiving. Every act of forgiveness, however small it might seem, is part of the healing of this earth and its people.

A Profile from Death Row

Warren McCleskey, an African American, became a Christian on Georgia's death row. He had been convicted of murdering a white police officer. McCleskey admitted taking part with three other men in the robbery of a furniture store, but denied shooting and killing the Atlanta police officer who responded to the alarm. The evidence supported McCleskey's claim, but at trial it was manipulated to the degree that he was found guilty and sentenced to death.

For the next thirteen years, McCleskey worked to have his conviction overturned. Twice his appeals went to the U.S. Supreme Court, where they were denied. In the meantime, McCleskey discovered Jesus Christ. His faith was strong. A life that had formerly been chaotic became centered on God.

The case of Warren McCleskey shows us two things: First, the criminal justice system makes mistakes. In the words of McCleskey's attorney, "His case from beginning to end illustrates the fallibility of the death penalty system." People are wrongfully convicted. Often those convicted in error are members of a minority group and are poor.

Second, even a convicted prisoner can undergo radical transformation and become a "new person." The Georgia director of the Southern Prison Ministry knew McCleskey for ten years. "The gift that Warren gave all of us was his dignity and inner peace," she said. "He taught me about a level of faith that I have not seen anywhere else."

On the morning he was executed, Warren McCleskey made a final statement that demonstrated the importance of his faith and the depth of the change he had undergone. First, he addressed the family of the police officer who had been killed:

> "I am deeply sorry and repentant for the suffering, hurt, and pain that you have endured over the years. . . . I pray that you would find in your heart to forgive me for the participation in crime that caused the loss of your loved one. I realize that the words that I am sharing with you now offer very little comfort; nevertheless, I want you to know that I have asked God to forgive me and pray in my heart that you will forgive me. . . ."

To his own family, he said:

> "Do not hold any bitterness toward anyone. . . . This is my request for you, that you be forgiving to all. And I pray that you will go on with your lives, and that you will keep God at the center. . . ."

(This profile is based on Joyce Hollyday, "A Gift of Dignity.")

Appendix D

Suicide: A Tragic Attack on Life

A sixteen-year-old girl, known for her flowing red hair and her constant smile, walks alone on a railroad track. It is early morning. The sky is blue, and the sun is shining. A train approaches, moving fast, right on schedule. The train's engineer sees the girl. He frantically pulls the cord that sets off the train's loud horn and applies the emergency brake; he knows he cannot stop the train in time. The girl is calm. She looks over her shoulder, sees the speeding train, and continues to walk in its path. Seconds later, she is dead.

Death is not always evaded and denied. Sometimes death is sought and found. Some lives are stressed to the breaking point. Like the girl on the tracks, many people are burdened with depression and despair, with financial and relational problems they cannot seem to solve, with wounds they cannot seem to heal. Too many carry their burdens alone.

The family and friends of the sixteen-year-old girl are shocked and broken by the news of her death. They shake their head and wring their hands: "Why did she have to do this? What drove her to it?"

Searching for a Cause

We cannot know for sure why any given individual chooses suicide. But clues always turn up, usually after the death. The girl killed on the tracks had left a suicide note that said: "How could you possibly love me? Please don't hate me for what I'm about to do." No one had ever before heard the dark cry hidden beneath her constant smile. She was calm in the face of death because, to her, death would be a relief. Her perception of reality had become distorted by her own self-hatred, isolation, and despair.

Intense Pain

People who move toward suicide are people who have been suffering intensely. Suicide is not the first despairing step a person takes, but the last in a long series of steps spiraling downward. Suicide is due not to a specific problem but to a complexity of interlocking problems that has become unbearable. Self-loathing and isolation do not come in a moment. They grow gradually, taking root over time, bringing a person's usual ways of coping to their limit.

Many people have the mistaken impression that if a person has committed suicide, he or she must have been insane. Most suicide victims are not insane; they are people with normal human capacities who at some point in life feel so isolated and unhappy that they can no longer cope. Their perception of themselves, of those around them, of God, and perhaps of life itself has become distorted, but this does not mean they are insane. The misconception that suicide is committed only by people who are insane is particularly harmful because it may prevent a suicidal person from reaching out for help. He or she may fear that, "They'll just think I'm crazy." But help and treatment *are* available for people who are depressed or having difficulty coping.

When the loved ones of a person who has committed suicide have gained some understanding of the possible reasons for the suicide, their next question is likely to be, "What could I have done to prevent this?"

Warning Signs

Almost every person who has ever committed or attempted to commit suicide has given warning signs. Some signs might be as direct as a statement:

"There's no way out of this depression" or "You'll be sorry after I'm dead." Other signs will be less obvious. The person may withdraw from family members and friends. Signs of depression may appear, such as a lack of enthusiasm about activities that have always been of interest, a loss of energy, changes in sleep patterns or appetite, a sudden weight gain or loss, or comments that reflect a negative self-image. A person who is close to suicide may give away things she or he owns. Sometimes people who have decided to attempt suicide go through an abrupt change of mood—from being extremely depressed to being at peace. A sudden mood change of this kind indicates a false sense of peace that has come from having finally made the decision to commit suicide. It does not indicate a genuine sense of peace from having solved a series of problems.

As time passes after the funeral of the girl on the railroad track, her family and friends begin to recognize warning signs they had not understood before. Her mother realizes that for several months before her death, her daughter had talked to her less. Her friends begin to understand why she had been ignoring them. Teachers think back to the look of fatigue evident in her face and posture, and the assignments she failed to complete. Her brother recalls that the night before she died she ate only half her dinner, then went to her room without saying anything. The next morning she ate breakfast cheerfully and left the house in a good mood.

By discovering and interpreting the warning signs they had previously missed, the family and friends of the red-haired girl gain an increased understanding of her suicide and the events leading up to it. This leaves them with a new responsibility: to grow more completely and compassionately aware of the day-to-day needs of those still living. And it leaves them with a vital challenge: to forgive themselves for whatever they failed to do, and to forgive her for what she chose to do.

The Voice of the Church

Catholic teaching asks us to trust that God's love and wisdom always prevail. It reminds us that we are cherished by a God who is merciful. The church teaches that it is because God loves us that God entrusts us with real responsibility. We are the stewards, or caretakers, of the life given to us by God. To deliberately end that life, therefore, violates the trust that God has placed in us.

Suicide is also a contradiction of the natural human tendency to love oneself and one's neighbor. The human inclination is to preserve one's own life. When we are ill, for example, we go to a doctor. This inclination is contradicted by suicide. Human beings are also inclined to reach out to their family and neighbors, but suicide breaks the individual away from family and community obligations. A parent who commits suicide, for instance, cannot fulfill his or her child-raising responsibility.

Catholic teaching both acknowledges the seriousness of suicide and roots itself in God's merciful love. Death, whether by suicide or by other causes, takes a person directly into God's loving presence. Nothing can destroy God's desire to bring us to joy. Family and friends of the red-haired girl may fear that she will be punished or condemned for the choice she made, that she will spend eternity in hell, completely apart from God. This is a common misunderstanding of Catholic teaching about suicide. Catholic faith holds firm to the belief that God's love for us does not come to an end, that the souls of suicide victims are entrusted to God and can be saved. The Christian community, bearing God's great compassion, prays for these victims and for those who love them.

Resolute as she walked along the tracks, the red-haired girl did not know that she was cherished—by family, friends, and God. She chose death, believing her problems to be insurmountable, her life worthless, herself unlovable. Where was God that day and all the days leading up to it?

Catholic faith says that God was with her all along, loving her as much as ever, each day allowing her complete freedom to make her own choices. Two things, given to her from the beginning, are hers forever: God's love and her free will. The same two gifts have been given to each of us.

Learning to Hear the Cries

Suicide occurs in all cultures, in every kind of family, among atheists and among believers, among the diseased and among the healthy, among the elderly and among the young, in all kinds of circumstances, from poverty to affluence. Those closest to the tragedy are always crushed with grief. They suffer the torments of powerlessness and rage. Sorrowful, they recognize the ways they have failed to love. Some blame themselves too much; others understand they did not have the power to prevent death.

By ending her life, the girl on the tracks moved out of the reach of physical human contact, but not beyond the reach of love and faith. She can still be touched by our prayers and our continuing commitment to live out our own life in love. We can learn to hear and respond to the unspoken cries of those around us. And we can learn to recognize and voice our own cries for support and help.

Appendix E

Death and the World's Religions

The sun has just begun to rise. A painter sets his easel on a sandy shore. He takes up his palette of blues, reds, and yellows and begins to paint a portrait of the dawn. Down the shore stands another painter. She too holds a palette of colors and is painting the dawn. Farther down stands a third painter, and a fourth and a fifth and a sixth. All along the shore are artists, each with a clean white canvas, all seeking to capture the dawn.

Each painter works from the same primary palette of blues, reds, and yellows. Each painter looks out over the one ocean and the one sky, watching the same sun rise. Each will finish with a portrait of the early morning dawn. But each painting will be somehow different from all the others.

This appendix provides thumbnail sketches of how four of the world's major religions, other than Christianity, approach death. Just as there are various ways of painting a sunrise, the religions of the world have developed various ways of understanding death. In a world characterized by religious diversity, these understandings need not put us at odds with one another. The Catholic approach to the reality of religious diversity is summarized in the final section of the appendix.

Hinduism

Hinduism is considered to be the world's oldest religion. It is practiced today by more than 700 million people in India and other countries.

Hinduism was not founded by a particular individual. Rather, it is an aggregate of thought systems coming from various sages, saints, mystics, and philosophers. Its development continues to this day.

Hinduism emphasizes that there is not just one spiritual path, but many. All these paths lead to the one God, though different traditions give God different names. For Hindus, the goal of all religion is to help us discover and live out the divinity already in us.

According to Hindu belief, the ultimate reality, the source of all, is called Brahman. Brahman is the ground of all existence. The goal of life is liberation—release from the suffering that permeates human life, along with the realization of the essential reality that is Brahman. In liberation, death is conquered by the revelation of the eternal nature of the soul.

The way to liberation is to let go of all earthly desires and fears, including fears about dying. Death must be faced and accepted as a necessary and inevitable part of the soul's journey to its final goal.

Most do not achieve liberation in a single lifetime. A cycle of successive deaths and rebirths is necessary and unavoidable. This process is known as reincarnation. After the physical death of one body, the individual soul moves on to a new body and continues the journey to liberation.

Rebirth is governed by the law of karma. The word *karma* means "action," and the law of karma holds that every action, good or bad, produces a result. Throughout life, every action contributes to the overall direction of a person's karma. At the time of death, this overall direction determines the condition of the next life. An individual who has done more good than bad in his or her lifetime moves closer to liberation, whereas an individual who has done more bad than good moves further away from liberation.

At death, the soul passes through an array of heavens and hells determined by past karma. After a period of purification, the soul is reborn in the form that it deserves—perhaps the form of a god, a human, or an animal. The Hindu scriptures describe the process with an analogy: The soul is like a rider, and the body is a chariot. At death, the rider changes from one chariot to another.

Hindu life is marked by a number of *samskaras,* or sacraments, that occur at moments like birth, marriage, and death. At a person's death, survivors perform rites for the future good of the deceased in the hope that she or he will one day achieve liberation. Traditional funerals last at least ten days, after which the deceased person becomes an "ancestor." Sacrifices are offered on anniversaries of the death and on other occasions, on behalf of the ancestor.

In Summary: Hinduism

- The afterlife is determined by the actions of a person throughout his or her life; therefore, life is of greater importance than the afterlife.
- Death is followed by the soul's rebirth in another body. Death is not the end.
- Death has meaning. It is a necessary part of the journey to liberation.
- Liberation is the realization that the soul is immortal. Immortality does not refer to the long sequence of rebirths of the soul into a series of bodies, but to the immortality of Brahman, which is the ground of all existence, human and otherwise.
- Everyone is destined to realize immortality.
- Fear of death is overcome by the reality of liberation.

Buddhism

Buddhism has its roots in Hinduism. Its founder was born into a Hindu family, but his path to enlightenment led him to break away from his religion of birth.

Siddhārtha Gautama was a rich young man, a prince. His father, the king, feared that Siddhārtha would turn his back on the worldly life if he ever witnessed the sufferings and hardships experienced by so many people in the world, so he kept Siddhārtha isolated from society. Siddhārtha inevitably caught sight of such realities—old age, disease, and death—and renounced his princely life. He took to the road to seek enlightenment. After six years of traveling and studying, he attained that goal and became known as the Buddha, which means "the Enlightened One."

At the heart of the Buddha's teachings are the Four Noble Truths. First, all of life involves suffering. Second, suffering is caused by desire and greed. Third, suffering will end when desire ends—that is, when a person stops being a slave to his or her desires. Fourth, following the Buddha's Eightfold Path is the way to end suffering.

The way out of suffering, then, is to free oneself from desire. Of course, we cannot be entirely free from desire. For example, hunger causes us to desire food, and parents desire good health for their children. Seeking to fulfill desire for the sake of desire itself, though, causes us to become attached to desire, and it is that attachment that must be eliminated if suffering is to come to an end. The Buddha's Eightfold Path provides guidelines about "right living" that help one attain enlightenment, which is freedom from attachment to desires.

Buddhism's belief about death is similar to that of Hinduism, but there are important differences. Hinduism teaches that at death, the individual soul goes through a period of purification before being reincarnated in a new body. The Buddha also taught that reincarnation occurs, but he denied that an individual soul passes to the new body. The Buddha rejected the idea of an individual soul, saying that what Hindus thought of as a soul was actually impermanent. What passes over in reincarnation is a pattern of character traits that is the product of the karma of all the past lives. It is like what passes from a flame when it is used to light a candle: the flame itself does not transfer, but its energy does.

In Buddhism, as in Hinduism, the law of karma operates automatically. Good actions produce positive results, bad actions produce negative ones, and at death the sum of a person's karma determines the nature of her or his rebirth. While living, any person can overcome her or his past karma through liberation from suffering. The law of karma is suspended in the case of a person who has achieved enlightenment, and when that person dies, she or he will not be reborn.

Judaism

For Jewish people, God is a creative presence. God is also a divine parent, both loving and just. Abraham, considered the father of the Jewish faith, received the first great revelation of God's personal and loving presence. God formed a covenant of love with Abraham: God would take care of the Hebrew people, blessing them richly; in return, they would believe in, love, and obey God. To worship God and carry out God's commandments is to find ever-deepening joy and fulfillment.

The purpose of life, in the Jewish view, is to give glory to God on earth by giving expression to one's higher, or spiritual, self by following the Ten Commandments. Made in God's image, Jews see themselves as called to turn away from evil and toward all that is good.

The Jewish view, based on the stories of Creation in the Hebrew Scriptures, is that death entered the world through sin, when Adam and Eve were disobedient in the Garden of Eden (see chapter 3 of the Book of Genesis). The root of that sin was lack of trust in God. Each person will be held accountable for acts here on earth. The faithful will be rewarded with eternal joy in heaven, and the wicked will suffer eternal punishment in hell.

Belief in life after death developed gradually in Jewish thought. Some Jews believe that immortality will bring about the resurrection of both body and soul. Others believe in the resurrection of the soul only. Still others do not believe in the afterlife at all.

In any case, Jewish thought is not preoccupied with the afterlife. The first and most important responsibility is to focus on fully living this life now, because all people will be accountable to God for how they live the life they were given.

The story of Abraham, who was willing to sacrifice his beloved son Isaac at God's request (although God did not require Abraham to complete the sacrifice), shows that faith in God transcends even the fear of death. The same confidence is found among the writers of the Psalms. The human cry of anguish is coupled with faith in the God who is present even in our suffering.

What does Judaism teach about the end of the world? Biblical accounts of the flood tell of God's promise to Noah that the world would never again be destroyed. In Jewish thought, this promise is taken literally. Accordingly, the earth will be not destroyed but changed. With this in mind, the Jewish people await the coming of a Messiah who will bring peace to the earth, a peace such as has never before been known. This long-awaited Messiah is expected to free people from all oppression. In the messianic age, death as we now know it will not exist. Sadness and sorrow will be no more. Through the resurrection of the body, all will be transformed and redeemed, both individually and collectively.

In the Jewish faith, the prescribed death rituals are developed in great detail. They serve two main purposes: to help the dead person move toward salvation, and to provide healing for those who are grieving. For example, during a seven-day period of deep mourning, called *shiv'ah*, mourners cease to participate in everyday activities. Instead, they pray, meditate, and read from the sacred books, and each day a family member says the *kaddish*, the mourner's prayer. The *kaddish* praises God and affirms faith in God, helping to lift the spirits of the mourners. The *kaddish* is also recited regularly for a full year, a practice that serves as a petition on behalf of the deceased person. Those who have lost a loved one are obligated to love, honor, and remember the deceased in an ongoing series of prayers and services.

In Summary: Judaism
- The purpose of life is to give glory to God.
- Death entered the world through sin.
- Belief in life after death was a gradual development in Jewish thought.
- The world will not end, but will be changed, in the messianic age.
- Some Jews believe that the body and soul will be resurrected; others believe that only the soul will be resurrected.
- Jewish death rituals intercede for the dead and help heal those who mourn.

Islam

Islam officially began as a religion around the year 622 in Arabia. Like Judaism and Christianity, Islam has its roots in the tradition of the patriarch Abraham, whose story is told in the Book of Genesis in the Hebrew Scriptures. These three religions also share the characteristic of being monotheistic, or believing in a single God. Today Islam is a worldwide faith comprising many varied sects and more than 950 million followers.

The primary belief of Islam is that Allah is the one and only God, and that Muhammad is Allah's prophet. The greatest sin in Islam is to recognize any god other than Allah. Muhammad, to whom the Islamic revelation was given, was born around 570. This revelation was written down in the Holy Qur'an (or Koran).

Followers of Islam (also called Muslims) recognize that God has an infinite number of attributes. For example, God is all-powerful, all-knowing, just, and merciful. God calls humans to live good, moral lives, and because humans are likely to make mistakes, the mercy of God is plentiful.

Accordingly, the Islamic faith emphasizes the concepts of human freedom and responsibility. These notions, however, are held in tension with the idea that humans can do little or nothing to alter the basic destiny God has predetermined for them.

For Muslims, human experience of Allah's creation does not end with death. Earthly life has only one purpose: to prepare a person to pass through death and to progress in the afterlife.

Dying persons are attended to by friends and relatives, and verses of the Qur'an are read. Death is believed to occur in the context of a personal encounter with an angel of death who has been sent by God. The separation of the soul from the body is considered to be an agonizing experience. The cessation of breathing is the visible sign of this experience.

Death marks the transition from this life into eternity. The Qur'an speaks of a barrier that separates the living from the dead; the soul of the deceased goes beyond the barrier and begins a period of waiting for final judgment. The deceased has no way to return to the earth. Each person has one earthly life, and that life determines the nature of the person's future existence.

There is much speculation in Islam about what occurs between an individual's death and the final day of judgment, but the Qur'an offers no clues. Muslims believe that individuals undergo the "trial of the grave," in which they are questioned by the angels Munkar and Nakir and receive a preview of their eternal destiny. Eventually the day of judgment will arrive, preceded by catastrophic events and a disruption of the natural order. God will be all that remains. Then all humans will be bodily resurrected and receive God's judgment, based on their earthly lives. Those who are guilty of sin but still have faith will fall into fire for a period of purification. Unbelievers, with no faith or good deeds, will fall into the fire forever. Those who have faith and are free of sin will enter a garden paradise and dwell there forever. Martyrs (persons who die while defending Islam, while making the pilgrimage to Islam's holy city, Mecca, or while reciting the Qur'an) are rewarded by being admitted to paradise immediately after death.

Islam affirms that the fruits of the actions of this earthly life will be reaped in the life to come. It demonstrates, too, a strong faith that God is just and merciful and will reward all accordingly.

In Summary: Islam
- God is just and merciful, and human beings have freedom and responsibility.
- The purpose of earthly life is to prepare persons for the afterlife.
- Death is the transition from earthly life to eternal life.
- After physical death, everyone awaits the final day of judgment, when all bodies will be resurrected and judgment will be passed by God.

Catholicism and Religious Diversity

These brief sketches of four of the world's religions show a great diversity of views on life and death. The Catholic church has long recognized the need for respect among the world's religious traditions.

Christians believe that God wants all people to find the truth and the way to it, because God wants all to have the very best that life can offer. God sent Jesus, God-in-person, and all the questions of the Christian find answers in him. For Christians, Jesus is the model of human living and dying, and God is the source of all goodness and the ultimate power over death.

At the same time, Catholic teaching holds that nothing that is holy or true in other religions is to be rejected. Recall the image of many artists. As each artist works, both joy and struggle are involved in trying to capture the dawn. Each painting is done passionately and lovingly, with a spirit of hope about the finished outcome. Any given artist may wander along the shore at times, glimpsing the work of fellow artists. In doing so, that artist may enrich or enhance her or his own perspective. Returning to her or his own canvas, that artist may paint more passionately, may see more deeply into the face of the dawn.

For similar reasons, Catholics need not fear or shun religious diversity. All peoples can enrich, challenge, and deepen their own religious views through dialog about their respective "portraits" of life and death.

We will find some profound differences: Hinduism and Buddhism teach that we are born again and again until we discover our true identity. Islam, Judaism, and Christianity teach that we are born once and die once.

We will also find some basic similarities: belief in the universal, God-given capacity for human transcendence; belief in the necessity of renouncing evil and doing good; belief in the fundamental goal of harmony with the divine and with the created order. In all the world's religions, we find a spirit of hope and a yearning for fulfillment.

Religious diversity is a reality, as is the need for worldwide fellowship among peoples. As the bishops of the Second Vatican Council pointed out, our prayers to God will not ring true as long as we treat any people disrespectfully, for *all* people are created in God's image (*Declaration on the Relation of the Church to Non-Christian Religions,* number 5).

The most important question for any of us is, How can I use my freedom to bring about good? And the particular question for a Christian is, How can I go about my living and my dying as Jesus himself did?

The sun rises for all of us. We are each given a place on the shore. Aware that we stand in mystery, we paint—also conscious that this shoreful of diversity reflects a basic freedom that itself is God-given.

Index

Italic numbers are references to photos.

A

abortion: confession of, 112–113; emotional pain of, 119–120, 158; funeral for, 127, 138–142, 150; guilt for, 113, 124, 140, 169; human dignity and, 182; physical symptoms from, 119, 155

Abraham, 193, 194

activity, 32, 99, 182

Adam, 193

advertising, 28, 30–31, 33

afterlife: in Catholic theology, 65; human growth in, 66; intuitive knowledge of, 69; Judgment Day and, 68; near-death experiences and, 85; in world religions, 191–195. *See also* resurrection

aged persons, 26–27, 181

AIDS (disease), 89–90

alcoholic intoxication, 182; driving and, 93–94, 108, 115, 116; and family dysfunction, 112

Allah, 194, 195

Allen, Woody, 73

aloneness: of Christ, 17, 137; denial of God and, 37; of mourners, 122; of murdered brother, 121; pain of, 150; personal renewal and, 128; of students, 38; suffering and, 120; suicide and, 188

Alzheimer's disease: freedom from, 133, 145; indignities of, 26; irrationality in, 108; prayer for, 117; progress of, 9

"Amazing Grace" (song), 74

angels, 194

anger: of basketball player, 17, 117, 128; of Christ, 12, 16; fading of, 111, 168; at father, 122; frustration and, 33; at God, 133, 137, 166, 167, 171; lessons from, 44; suicide and, 190; of surviving twin, 134–135, 164–167, 168; violent death and, 64

animals, 32

Anointing of the Sick, sacrament of, 159–160, 162, 166–167, 169, 172

antimony, 140

anxiety. *See* fear

Apostles, 53

appearance, personal, 27, 28

artificial respiration, 180

artists, 86, 87, *157*

aspirin, 31

atheism, 162

automobile accidents: discussion of, 108–109, 110; immediate consequences of, 95, 132; news reporting of, 34; quadriplegia from, 180; responsibility for, 115

autumn, 142

avoidance. *See* denial

B

bacterial pneumonia, 155

Baptism, sacrament of, 47

barbiturates, 134

basketball, 10, 14, 95, 132

beatific vision. *See* heaven

beauty, physical, 27, 28

belief. *See* faith

bereavement. *See* grief

Berrigan, Daniel, 90

birth, 41–42, 80–81

Blessed Mother, 156, *157*

blindness, 82

bodily resurrection. *See* resurrection

Brahman, 191, 192

brain damage, 95. *See also* Alzheimer's disease

brain death, 87

Buddhism, 192–193, 195

Buechner, Frederick, 173–174

busyness, 32, 99, 182

C

Callahan, Daniel, 181

Canadian Senate, 181

cancer: 23, 29, 47, 50, 55, 178–179, 180

candles: in campus office, 105; at christenings, 47; in drama, 73, 74; at Easter, 51, 174; at funerals, 48–49, 51, 58; at prayer service, 138–139, 140–141, 150, 161

capital punishment, 184–187

car accidents. *See* automobile accidents

cardiac infarction, 88–89

catharsis. *See* emotional healing

Catholic theology. *See* Roman Catholic theology

cerebral palsy, 180

chemistry examinations, 14

childbirth, 41–42, 80–81

children, 83, 189, 192

chocolate: desire for, 77, 78–79; at grief-support meetings, 106, 149–150; overconsumption of, 81; popularity of, 80

christening, 47

Christian Testament. *See under individual books, for example,* Colossians, Letter to

Christmas, 173–174

collective power, 24–26

Colossians, Letter to, 177

commercials, 28, 33

Communion, 53, 56–57, 163, 168

communion of saints, 147, 172

communities, 24–26, 179

compassion: of caretakers, 179; euthanasia and, 182–183; freedom through, 141; of God, 101; and grief, 151; for suicide victims, 189; of teachers, 151

confidentiality, 106

Constitution, 184

consumerism, 28, 33, 192, 193

Corinthians, First Letter to, 68, 74

Corinthians, Second Letter to, 75

corpses, 28, 57, 68, 69

courage: admiration for, 150; of AIDS patient, 90; at Communion, 53; faith and, 39, 82; prayer for, 121

Courage to Grieve, The (Tatelbaum), 131

Creation story, 193

creativity, 26

criminal justice system, 184–185, 187

criminal reform, 184, 185

crisis response teams, 96

crucifixion, 10

crying: by Christ, 52; in group meetings, 113, 137; healing through, 108; indulgence in, 100, 169; repression of, 23, 29, 97

cultural attitudes: on aging, 26–27; on beauty, 28; Christian doctrine and, 38–39, 41; collective power and, 24–25; development of, 22; on emotional pain, 29, 30; on euthanasia, 183; operation of, 32–33; on talking, 106

cynicism, 137, 162

D

daisies, 164, 173

deafness, 83

death penalty, 184–187

Declaration on the Relation of the Church to Non-Christian Religions (Vatican Council II), 195

de Mille, Agnes, 7

denial: of aging, 27–28; collective power of, 25; consequences of, 37; of death, 21–22; of emotional pain, 29, 31, 98; family reinforcement of, 101; guilt and, 116; laughter and, 58; ongoing, 97; self-help programs and, 35; silence as, 32; sudden tragedy and, 96

Deploration of Christ (Nauen), *157*

depression: appetite and, 112; drug abuse and, 31; euthanasia and, 180, 181; suicide and, 188, 189; "tastes" of death and, 80. *See also* manic-depressive illness

Descent from the Cross (W. H. Johnson), *157*

desire, 77–82, 192, 193

despair, 44, 75, 80, 171, 188

deterrence, 185

Deuteronomy, Book of, 69

dialysis, 180

Dickinson, Emily, 86

dignity, 182, 183, 185

distraction, 32, 34

diversity, 195

divorce, 23, 112

dramatic productions, 25–26, 70–75

drugs. *See* medications

drunkenness. *See* alcoholic intoxication

E

Easter, 70, 174

Easter candle, 51

Easter Proclamation, 174

Eden, 193

Eightfold Path, 192, 193

elderly persons, 26–27, 181

electroencephalograms, 87

Emmaus, 72, 73, 75

emotional healing, 108, 131, 137, 148, 172. *See also* health

emotional pain: of abortion, 119–120, 158; denial of, 29, 31; expression of, 166; need for, 44; numbing of, 98; suppression of, 100–101, 125, 161; unpredictability of, 111. *See also* depression; grief; suffering

empathy. *See* compassion

enlightenment, 192, 193

Ephesians, Letter to the, 82, 159

eternal life. *See* afterlife; resurrection

Eucharist, sacrament of, 53, 56–57, 163, 168

euphemisms, 32

euthanasia, 180–183

Eve, 193

executions, 184–187

exhaustion, 39, 124

Exsultet, 174

F

faith: action on, 52; assurance of, 90; constancy in, 18; courage and, 39, 82; devaluation of, 37; of disciples, 73; exhortation to, 50; fear transformed to, 44; at funerals, 57; hope and, 39, 41, 82; inner confusion and, 132; Jewish teaching on, 193; joy from, 43; Muslim teaching on, 194, 195; peace and, 187; prayer for, 45; in resurrection, 133; "tastes" of death and, 80; weak, 40, 41, 162, 163, 172
fall season, 142
families, 83, 178, 189, 192
Farewell to Arms, A (Hemingway), 127
fatigue, 39, 124
fear: of death, 22, 37, 39–40, 85; of further loss, 114; of God, 153, 158, 169; paralyzing, 171; shared, 7; transformed, 44; truth and, 41
final conversations, 135, 141–142
fitness, 27, 28
flowers, 42, 52–53, 164, 173. *See also* roses
food, 27, 31, 192. *See also* chocolate
football, 33
forgiveness: of Christ, 17–18; of God, 159, 186; in relationships, 42–43, 44, 128; requests for, 60; for suicide, 189; of unborn child, 124
Four Noble Truths, 192
Franke, Bob, 153
freedom: 66, 190; in counseling program, 106; from death, 69; Eastern teaching on, 191, 192; Muslim teaching on, 194, 195; revenge and, 184
friends, 11, 24, 43
funeral homes, 28

Funeral Rites, 128, 129
funerals: 127, 131–133, 192; for aborted baby, 138–142, 145, 150; for cancer victim, 47–61; for suicide victim, 134, 135

G

Gallup polls, 177
Garden of Eden, 193
Gautama, Siddhārtha, 192
Genesis, Book of, 182, 193, 194
Gide, André, 86
"Gift of Dignity, A" (Hollyday), 187
God: ambivalence about, 38, 131–132; anger at, 133, 137, 166, 167, 171; call of, 69; cancer and, 50; Catholic teaching on, 195; companionship of, 49; compassion of, 101; creation by, 45, 81; denial of, 37; dependence on, 117, 156; despair and, 75, 188; faith in (*see* faith); fear of, 153, 158, 169; forgiveness of, 159, 186; grace of, 9, 44, 68; guidance of, 129; human desire and, 81–82; images of, 182, 195; Jewish teaching on, 193–194; judgment by, 65, 66, 67–68, 194, 195; Kingdom of, 96; laughter at, 51; meeting with, 183; Muslim teaching on, 194, 195; near-death experiences and, 85; peace of, 149; prayer to (*see* prayer); providence of, 146; questions about, 22, 43–44, 148; sacraments and, 159–160; salvation of, 68, 175, 193; suicide and, 189–190; "tastes" of death and, 80–81; transformations by, 42, 44; unseen presences and, 147; will of, 16, 53–54. *See also* Jesus Christ

Gogh, Vincent van, *86*
good-byes, 141–142
Good Grief (Westberg), 130
Gospel of Life, The (John Paul II), 181–182, 183, 185
Gospels, 12–13, 50, 177. *See also* John, Gospel of; Luke, Gospel of; Mark, Gospel of; Matthew, Gospel of
grace, 9, 44, 68
greed, 28, 33, 192, 193
grief: for accident victims, 96; compassion and, 151; cultural denial and, 37; of disciples, 74; discussion of, 106; dual aspects of, 111; at funerals, 48, 49; grace and, 9; guilt and, 109; health and, 125; inevitability of, 21; journal writing and, 148; laughter and, 58; new relationships and, 162; powerlessness in, 156; questions raised by, 43–44; for self, 165; Shakespeare on, 93, 106; shared, 143; special occasions and, 70; stages of, 128–129, 130, 131; of suicide survivors, 190; unresolved, 54–55, 161; unseen presences and, 147; unselfishness and, 134. *See also* depression; emotional pain
Grief: The Mourning After (Sanders), 131
grief-work: beginning of, 97–101; commitment to, 118, 124; dependence in, 141; funeral memories and, 127; intensity of, 114; research on, 129; unpreparedness for, 96
guilt: for abortion, 113, 124, 140, 169; of accident survivors, 115, 116; at funerals, 60, 141, 145; healthy and unhealthy, 109; of surviving twin, 109, 110, 137
Gunning, Dr. Karel, 181

H

Habakkuk, Book of, 70
hairstyles: of accident survivor, 97; of twins, 100, 109, 110, 119, 124–125, 136
hallucinations, 85, 147
health, 125, 192. *See also* emotional healing
health care, 177, 180, 181
heart disease, 88–89
heaven, 133, 163, 172; Catholic teaching on, 65, 66, 67; Hindu teaching on, 191; Jewish teaching on, 193; Muslim teaching on, 194
Hebrews, Book of, 13
Hebrew Scriptures, 193, 194. *See also under individual books, for example,* Isaiah, Book of
Heil, Joyce, 178–179
hell, 65, 66, 191, 193, 194
Hemingway, Ernest, 130
Hinduism, 191–192, 195
holiness, 67
Hollyday, Joyce, 187
Holy Qur'an, 194
Holy Spirit, 129. *See also* God; Jesus Christ
Holy Week, 70
home care, 90, 177–179
homeless persons, 155
homicide, 182, 184, 185, 187
hope: candlelight symbolic of, 48; despair transformed into, 44; of disciples, 72; faith and, 39, 41, 82; at funerals, 49, 57, 60; loss of, 156; promises supporting, 43; in resurrection, 57, 60, 75, 133; sand picture symbolic of, 158; in world religions, 195
hopelessness, 44, 75, 80, 171, 188
hospice care, 90, 177–179, 180

Host (Eucharist), 53, 57, 163, 168
human corpses, 28, 57, 68, 69
human desire, 77–82, 192, 193
human dignity, 182, 183, 185
human freedom, 66, 190. *See also* freedom
human limitations, 35, 38, 101, 156. *See also* emotional pain; vulnerability
human transcendence, 195
humor, 32, 90

I

illness, 125, 166; manic-depressive, 63, 64, 108, 117, 172; terminal, 177–183. *See also* Anointing of the Sick, sacrament of
immediacy, 33
immortality. *See* afterlife; resurrection
incense, 57
innocence, 10, 22
insanity, 188
instant gratification, 33
intercessory prayer, 53
intoxication. *See* alcoholic intoxication
Isaac, 193
Isaiah, Book of, 51, 139, 140, 148, 149
Islam, 194–195
isolation. *See* aloneness

J

James, Letter of, 163
Jeremiah, Book of, 149
Jesus Christ: aloneness of, 17, 137; Catholic teaching on, 195; Communion with, 53, 56–57, 168; death of, 19, 42, 82; encouragement by, 50; faith in, 133, 187; forgiveness

of, 17–18; on fruitfulness, 86; funerals and, 48–49, 60; grief of, 120, 136; human hungers and, 81; humanness of, 12–13; on joy, 43; at Last Judgment, 68; laughter at, 51; law of, 185–186; love of, 19; mother of, 156, *157;* mystery of, 10, 11; Nativity of, 173–174; peace of, 55; Peter and, 16, 17; in school drama, 70–75; sick persons and, 159–160, 163; storm calmed by, 8, 9, 37–38, 39–41; student knowledge of, 9–11, 15, 38; suffering of, 16, 38, 182; unbounded love through, 142; unification with, 68, 172; weeping by, 52. *See also* God; Holy Spirit
John, Gospel of: on eternal life, 74; on fruitfulness, 38, 86; on future joy, 43; on heaven, 163; on Lazarus, 52; on light of life, 49
John Paul II, Pope, 182–183, 185
Johnson, William H., *157*
journal writing, 148–149
Judaism, 193–194, 195
Judgment Day, 67–68, 194, 195
justice system, 184–185, 187

K

kaddish, 193–194
karma, 191, 192, 193
King John (Shakespeare), 93
kissing, 77–78, 79, 90
Koran, 194

L

Lamentation (W. H. Johnson), *157*
Lamentations, Book of, 174

physicians: death certification by, 87; euthanasia and, 180, 181; hospice teams and, 178; sedation by, 90; visits to, 189

Pietà, 156, *157*

plays, 25–26, 70–75

pneumonia, 155

poets, 86, 87

police, 155, 187

poor defendants, 184, 187

poppies, 42

prayer: of Christ, 13; communion of saints and, 147; for courage, 121; disrespect and, 195; doubt and, 162, 173, 175; enraged, 137; funeral, 57; in hospital, 159, 163, 166, 167, 168; intercessory, 53; Jewish, 193–194; Lord's, 168, 186; resentment of, 130; in school, 104; Tennyson on, 160; for trust, 45

pregnancy, 119, 127. *See also* abortion; childbirth

professionals, 85, 129, 130

promiscuity, 182

Psalms, Book of, 52, 69, 74, 86, 151, 168, 193

psychological experts, 85

public safety, 185

purgatory, 65, 67

pyxes, 163, 168

Q

quadriplegia, 180

Qur'an, 194

R

rage. *See* anger

Raymond, Rossiter Worthington, 63

rehabilitation, 184, 185

reincarnation, 191, 192, 193, 195

religious diversity, 195

religious orders, 177

remorse. *See* guilt

resurrection, 82; birth as, 41–42; in daily life, 43; foretastes of, 37; hope in, 57, 60, 75, 133; Jewish teaching on, 193, 194; Muslim teaching on, 194, 195; questions about, 44; in school drama, 70–75; sharing in, 182; unknown nature of, 65; vestments symbolic of, 48. *See also* afterlife

Revelation, Book of, 75

revenge, 12, 18, 184, 185, 186

rights, 180

Rilke, Rainer Maria, 91, 157, 162

rite of committal, 60

rocks, 27

Roman Catholic theology: on afterlife, 65, 66–67; on capital punishment, 185; on communion of saints, 147; on euthanasia, 181–182; on religious diversity, 195; on suicide, 189–190

Romans, Letter to the, 68, 133, 164

roses, 113–114, 138–139, 140, 143–145, 150

rubies, 140

rumors, 23, 24, 25

S

sacraments. *See* Anointing of the Sick, sacrament of; Baptism, sacrament of; Eucharist, sacrament of; *samskaras*

sacrifices, 192

Saint-Exupéry, Antoine de, 38

salvation, 68, 175, 193. *See also* heaven

samskaras, 192

Sanders, Catherine M., 131

sapphires, 140

Satan, 16, 17

Saunders, Cicely, 177, 179

Schopenhauer, Arthur, 37

Second Vatican Council, 195

sedation, 90

self-destruction. *See* suicide

self-disclosure, 137

self-esteem, 128

self-hatred, 188, 189

self-help books, 35

self-interest, 183

self-sufficiency, 97, 140

senior citizens, 26–27, 181

senses, 144

sexual intimacy: Christ and, 13; controls on, 82; desire for, 79, 80; illicit, 119, 182

Shakespeare, William, 93, 106

shame. *See* guilt

shiv'ah, 193

shock, 96, 98

shopping malls, 33

sickness. *See* illness

Siddhārtha Gautama, 192

Sign of Peace, 55, 59

silence, 32, 33, 34

sin, 193, 194

skepticism, 137, 162

social attitudes. *See* cultural attitudes

Song of Songs, 164, 170

soul, 192, 194

sound systems, 77, 78

Southern Prison Ministry, 187

Starry Night, The (van Gogh), 86

Stoddard, Sandol, 90

Acknowledgments

The scriptural quotations on page 19, the third and fourth quotes on page 52, the second quote on page 69, the quote on page 82, the first quote on page 86, and the quote on page 101 are from the New American Bible with revised Psalms and revised New Testament. Copyright © 1986, 1991 by the Confraternity of Christian Doctrine, 3211 Fourth Street NE, Washington, DC 20017. All rights reserved. Used with permission.

The scriptural quotations on pages 39, 49, the second quote on page 68, the first quote on page 69, the first quote on page 75, and the quotes on pages 139, 159, 168, and 177 are from the New Jerusalem Bible. Copyright © 1985 by Darton Longman and Todd, London, and Doubleday, a division of Bantam Doubleday Dell Publishing Group, New York. All rights reserved. Reprinted by permission.

The scriptural quotations on pages 10, 43, 70, the second quote on page 75, the second quote on page 86, and the quotes on pages 140, 170, 174, and 182 are from the New Revised Standard Version of the Bible. Copyright © 1989 by the Division of Christian Education of the National Council of the Churches of Christ in the United States of America. All rights reserved.

The scriptural quotations on pages 13, 38, 51, the first two quotes on page 52, the first quote on page 68, the quotes on pages 120, 133, 148, 149, 151, the first quote on page 163, and the quotes on page 164 are from the Revised English Bible. Copyright © 1989 by Oxford University and Cambridge University Presses. All rights reserved. Used with permission.

All other scriptural quotations in this book are freely adapted and are not to be understood or used as official translations of the Bible.

page 7:
The epigraph is from *Reprieve: A Memoir,* by Agnes de Mille (Garden City, NY: Doubleday and Company, 1981), page 41. Copyright © 1981 by Agnes de Mille.

page 21:
The epigraph is by Somerset Maugham, as quoted in *A Rumor of Angels,* edited by Gail Perry and Jill Perry (New York: Ballantine Books, 1989), page 68. Copyright © 1989 by Gail Perry and Jill Perry.

page 22:
The quote by Woody Allen is reprinted from *A Rumor of Angels,* page 73.

The quote by Margaret Mead is reprinted from *A Rumor of Angels,* page 66.

page 37:
The epigraph is by Arthur Schopenhauer, as quoted in *A Rumor of Angels,* page 174.

page 38:
The excerpt by Antoine de Saint-Exupéry is reprinted from *A Rumor of Angels,* page 81.

page 47:
The epigraph is by Anne Morrow Lindbergh, as quoted in *A Rumor of Angels,* page 110.

The quotes from the funeral Mass are adapted from the English translation of the *Rite of Funerals.* Copyright © 1970 by the International Committee on English in the Liturgy (ICEL). All rights reserved.

pages 49, 50:
The entrance song excerpts are from "Be Not Afraid," by Robert J. Dufford, SJ. Copyright © 1975, 1978 by Robert J. Dufford and New Dawn Music, 5536 NE Hassalo, Portland, OR 97213. All rights reserved. Used with permission.

pages 53, 55, 56:
The quotes from the Rite of the Eucharist are from the English translation of the *Roman Missal.* Copyright © 1973 by the ICEL. All rights reserved. Used with permission.

page 55:
The lyrics of "Peace Is Flowing Like a River" are reprinted from *Rise Up Singing: The Group-Singing Song Book,* conceived, developed, and edited by Peter Blood and Annie Patterson (Bethlehem, PA: Sing Out, 1988), page 195. Copyright © 1988, 1992 by Sing Out Corporation.

page 56:
"Amazing Grace" was written by John Newton.

page 57:
The quote from the funeral Mass is adapted from the English translation of the *Rite of Funerals.*

pages 58, 59:

The closing song "How Can I Keep from Singing?" is a Quaker hymn reprinted from *Music Issue 1991,* edited by John J. Limb (Portland, OR: Oregon Catholic Press, 1991), number 230. Copyright © 1991 by Oregon Catholic Press. Used with permission.

page 63:

The epigraph is by Rossiter Worthington Raymond, as quoted in *A Rumor of Angels,* page 144.

page 77:

The epigraph is by a survivor of the Belsen concentration camp, as quoted in *A Rumor of Angels,* page 20.

pages 84–85:

The story about the seventh-grade boy is from *Transformed by the Light: The Powerful Effect of Near-Death Experiences on People's Lives,* by Melvin L. Morse, MD. Copyright © 1992 by Melvin L. Morse. Reprinted by permission of Villard Books, a division of Random House.

page 86:

The quote by Emily Dickinson is from *The Letters of Emily Dickinson,* edited by Thomas H. Johnson (Cambridge, MA: Harvard University Press, 1958), page 332. Copyright © 1914, 1924, 1932 by Martha Dickinson Bianchi. Copyright © 1958 by the President and Fellows of Harvard College.

The quote by Vladimir Nabokov is reprinted from *A Rumor of Angels,* page 143.

The quote by André Gide is reprinted from *A Rumor of Angels,* page 171.

The quote by Vincent van Gogh is from *Dear Theo: The Autobiography of Vincent van Gogh,* edited by Irving Stone (Boston: Houghton Mifflin, and Cambridge, MA: Riverside Press, 1937), page 427. Copyright © 1937 by Irving Stone.

pages 87, 89:

The excerpts by Dr. Sherwin Nuland are from *How We Die: Reflections on Life's Final Chapter* (New York: Alfred A. Knopf, 1994), pages 123 and 5. Copyright © 1993 by Sherwin B. Nuland. Used with permission of Random House.

page 88:

The information about the death of Mrs. Nouwen is from *In Memoriam,* by Henri J. M. Nouwen (Notre Dame, IN: Ave Maria Press, 1980). Copyright © 1980 by Ave Maria Press.

page 90:

The excerpt by Fr. Daniel Berrigan is from *Sorrow Built a Bridge: Friendship and AIDS* (Baltimore: Fortkamp Publishing, 1989), page 14. Copyright © 1989 by Fortkamp Publishing, Marion, South Dakota. Reprinted with permission of Fortkamp Publishing.

The excerpt by Sandol Stoddard is from *The Hospice Movement: A Better Way of Caring for the Dying* (Briarcliff Manor, NY: Stein and Day Publishers, 1978), page 52. Copyright © 1978 by Sandol Stoddard.

page 91:

The poem by Rainer Maria Rilke is from *Rainer Maria Rilke: Selected Poems,* translated by Albert Ernest Flemming (New York: Routledge, 1990), page 56. Translations copyright © 1983, 1985 by Albert Ernest Flemming. Used with permission of Routledge, New York.

page 93:

The epigraph is from *King John,* by William Shakespeare, act 3, scene 4, line 93. Reprinted from *The Oxford Dictionary of Quotations,* fourth edition, edited by Angela Partington (New York: Oxford University Press, 1992), page 594. Copyright © 1979, 1992 by Oxford University Press.

page 103:

The epigraph is by Marilee Zdenek, as quoted in *A Rumor of Angels,* page 99.

page 106:

The excerpt by William Shakespeare is from *Macbeth,* act 4, scene 3, line 208. Reprinted from *The Oxford Dictionary of Quotations,* page 604.

page 127:

The epigraph is from *A Farewell to Arms,* by Ernest Hemingway, as quoted in *A Rumor of Angels,* page 110.

page 130:

The ten-stage approach to grieving is summarized from *Good Grief: A Constructive Approach to the Problem of Loss,* by Granger E. Westberg (Philadelphia: Fortress Press, 1962). Copyright © 1962, 1971 by Fortress Press.

page 131:

The five-phase approach to grieving is summarized from *Grief: The Mourning After: Dealing with Adult Bereavement,* by Catherine M. Sanders (New York: John Wiley and Sons, 1989). Copyright © 1989 by John Wiley and Sons.

The three-phase approach to grieving is summarized from *The Courage to Grieve,* by Judy Tatelbaum (New York: Lippincott and Crowell, Publishers, 1980). Copyright © 1980 by Judith Tatelbaum.

page 153:

The epigraph is from the song "The Great Storm Is Over," by Bob Franke, reprinted from *Rise Up Singing,* page 116.

pages 157, 162:

The poems "Pietà" and "Foreboding," by Rainer Maria Rilke, are from *Rainer Maria Rilke,* pages 141 and 67. Used with permission of Routledge.

page 160:

The quote by Alfred Lord Tennyson is from *Idylls of the King,* "The Passing of Arthur," line 414, as quoted in *The Oxford Dictionary of Quotations,* page 682.

page 174:

The quote by Frederick Buechner is from *The Hungering Dark* (San Francisco: Harper and Row, Publishers, 1969), page 51. Copyright © 1969 by Frederick Buechner.

The quote by Alfred Lord Tennyson is from the prologue to *In Memoriam,* as quoted in *The Oxford Dictionary of Quotations,* page 682.

The Easter Proclamation is from the English translation of the *Rite of Holy Week,* copyright © 1972 by the ICEL. Used with permission.

page 175:

The untitled poem is by Mary Marrocco. Used with permission.

page 177:

The quote from a hospice patient is reprinted from a booklet published by Winona Area Hospice Services, Winona, Minnesota.

The quote by Cicely Saunders is from a brochure published by Winona Area Hospice Services, Winona, Minnesota.

The statistic about the number of hospices in the United States was taken from "A Family Guide to Hospice Care," by Francesca L. Kritz, *Good Housekeeping,* February 1995, page 178.

The Gallup poll statistic is from "A Guide to Hospice Care," by Katie Baer, *Harvard Health Letter,* April 1993, page 9.

page 178:

The information about the goals and methods of hospice care is from *In the Light of Dying: The Journals of a Hospice Volunteer,* by Joan Leslie Taylor (New York: Continuum Publishing Company, 1993), page xiii. Copyright © 1989 by Joan Leslie Taylor. Used with permission of the Crossroad Publishing Company.

page 179:

The quote by Cicely Saunders is from a brochure published by Winona Area Hospice Services, Winona, Minnesota.

page 181:

The two excerpts by Daniel Callahan are from *The Troubled Dream of Life: Living with Mortality* (New York: Simon and Schuster, 1993), pages 112–113 and 114. Copyright © 1993 by Daniel Callahan. Used with permission of the publisher.

The excerpts by Karel Gunning are from "Euthanasia Opens Door to Misuse, MD Says," *Toronto Globe and Mail,* 30 September 1994, no page.

pages 181, 182, 183:

The excerpts from *The Gospel of Life,* numbers 65 and 66, are quoted from *Origins,* 6 April 1995, pages 712 and 713.

page 185:

The excerpts by the U.S. bishops are from the *U.S. Bishops' Statement on Capital Punishment,* by the United States Catholic Conference (USCC) (Washington, DC: USCC, 1980), pages 5 and 7. Copyright © 1980 by the USCC, Washington, DC 20017. Used with permission. All rights reserved.

The excerpts from *The Gospel of Life,* numbers 56 and 9, are quoted from *Origins,* 6 April 1995, pages 709 and 693.

page 187:

The excerpt is from "A Gift of Dignity: The Story of Warren McCleskey," by Joyce Hollyday, *Sojourners,* January 1992, pages 25–26. Reprinted with permission from *Sojourners,* 2401 Fifteenth Street NW, Washington, DC 20009; 202-328-8842; fax 202-328-8757.

page 195:

The excerpt is from *Declaration on the Relation of the Church to Non-Christian Religions,* number 5, as quoted in *Vatican Council II: The Conciliar and Post Conciliar Documents,* edited by Austin Flannery, OP (Northport, NY: Costello Publishing Company, 1975), page 742. Copyright © 1975, 1984, and 1987 by Harry J. Costello and Reverend Austin Flannery.

Photo Credits

Page 157:

Artwork by Taeko Tomiyama: Asian Christian Art Association, Kyoto, Japan

Artwork by Heinrich Nauen: Erich Lessing, Art Resource, NY

Artwork by Michelangelo Buonarrotti: SuperStock, Inc., Jacksonville, FL

Artwork by William H. Johnson: National Museum of American Art, Washington, D.C., Art Resource, NY